Fish Don't Think

How to Catch Fish using a Fly and Bubble

Bob Kayne

Illustrations by Cathy Pennak

SunShine Press Publications

SunShine Press Publications, Inc.,
PO Box 333
Hygiene, CO 80533
www.sunshinepress.com

Cover design by Bob Schram of Bookends
Illustrations by Cathy Pennak
Cover photo by Jack Hofer

First Edition

Publisher's Cataloging-in-Publication Data

Kayne, Robert R.
    Fish don't think: how to catch fish using
a fly and bubble / Bob Kayne. — 1st ed.
    p. cm.
    Preassigned LCCN: 95-73244
    ISBN 1-888604-02-6

    1. Fishing rods. 2. Fly fishing. 3. Fishing
I. Title.

SH447.H46 1998   688.7'9

Printed in the United States

5 4 3 2 1

Printed on recycled acid-free paper using soy ink

Dedication

To Mr. Sigmund Kayne, who took me hunting and fishing when other fathers left their sons at home, and to my youngest son, Gregory Sigmund Kayne, who was my constant fishing, hunting and camping companion from the time we shared a sleeping bag when he was an infant and continued until he went to college. I think of them and miss them every time I go fishing.

Table of Contents

Illustrations

Introduction

The month was July, the year 1957, my second summer in Colorado. Jim and I were traveling the old forest service road up the Middle St. Vrain Creek heading to Lower Coney Lake. We broke off west on an old logging road which had been swept clean of soil and deeply rutted by years of cascading water. I had to work my four wheel drive Travelall around the huge boulders and across the exposed rock slabs in the road. When we got to Coney Creek, the water was running too deep and swift for the vehicle to cross. Off came the shoes and socks, on went the backpacks. We forded the creek; put on our shoes and socks and started up the faint trail at about the 9,000 ft. level. Lower Coney Lake was three-quarters of a mile away through the trees and then a climb of another 600 ft. in altitude. The high mountain lake lay right at timberline. The last 200 yards required us to climb up a 40 degree slope. As we reached the top of the slope, we looked down and saw the clear blue water of Coney Lake in the Alpine meadow below.

The year before, I had joined a local game and fish club. It was a volunteer group of sportsmen who stocked some of the high mountain lakes with the aid of the Colorado State Game and Fish Department. The State provided the fish, backpacks and identified the lakes that we were to stock. In those days these high lakes were stocked by carrying a five gallon can on your back on an old Marine metal framed backpack. Each backpack can contained four gallons of water and approximately five hundred native cutthroat trout fry. What an exciting time, living in Colorado, hiking in the mountains and carrying fish to stock a high mountain lake.

The club member's line of jeeps had started early in the morning and did not reach the trail head until early afternoon. We had to stop at almost every stream and trickle of water changing the water in the five gallon cans to replenish the oxygen supply for the fish.

Out of breath and gasping for air at 9,600 feet altitude we wanted to collapse, but first most of the cans full of fish were laid in the lake with the lids open so that the fry could work their way out into the cold, clear, blue water. We all sat or lay in the grass trying to get some air in the thin atmosphere.

The trip coordinator called out his need for five men to volunteer to hike to Upper Coney Lake. Being a flatlander, young, foolish and not knowing what I was getting into, I immediately volunteered. The next two hours were spent fighting through buck brush and across rock slides. Finally, completely exhausted we reached Upper Coney Lake and laid our cans in the shallows for the cutthroat fry to work their way out. Five of us had carried cans full of fish and water. The sixth person carried all the fishing tackle for the six of us.

I laid down on a large flat slab of rock overlooking the lake. Looking face up to the sky there were large black spots before my eyes with blue sky between the spots. The altitude had gotten to me and I did not want to move. Than I heard a shout, "I got one on". The adrenaline started to flow and the black spots suddenly disappeared. It is amazing what happens to the human body when it is excited. Sitting on the rock I put together my fly rod. Just sitting up made me dizzy and I did not yet risk standing. Finally I stood up and made a few casts with my fly rod without success, but I did see one very large cutthroat approach my fly floating on the surface. It looked at the fly and turned away. The coordinator called out, "It's time to head back. It's going to be dark pretty soon and this is a rough place to get out of after dark."

When we got back down to Lower Coney the rest of the crew were also packing up their gear and getting ready to go down the mountain. Looking back on Lower Coney we could see fish rising in the middle of the lake well beyond our ability to reach with the equipment available at that time. This was my first opportunity since the stocking trip of the year before to go back to Lower Coney Lake and fish.

Jim and I arrived at Lower Coney about 1:00 in the afternoon and looked out upon this beautiful, pristine Colorado mountain lake. The lake is approximately two hundred yards across and probably three hundred yards long, approximately twelve acres. Formed by ancient glaciers, the west end is at the base of a very steep rise and deep. The lake slowly gets shallower as you travel east. The east end is spotted with large rocks. Many are rising out of the water. It is possible to step from dry rock to dry rock and get fifty to one hundred feet out into the lake.

Looking down between the rocks you would think you could just wade out into the water and fish. Not only is this treacherous because of the jaggedness of the rocks, but it is difficult to determine if the water is one foot deep or five feet deep. The water is as clear as fine crystal.

After catching our breath and taking a bite of lunch, we carefully moved from rock to rock working out as far onto the lake as we could. With our fly rods we started to cast our flies. As is usual in high country fishing, no fish were working. There was no reason to believe that even one of those 5,000 fry we had put into that lake the year before had survived. Tiring of the fruitless fishing we worked our way back to the shore and proceeded to admire the scenery.

About the time the sun touched the mountain peaks to the west, there was a swirl in the middle of the lake. More swirls and dimples appeared. There were fish in the lake, and they were beginning to rise. Hastily, we worked our way back out onto the rocks and tried to reach them. Our fly rods were useless in that these fish were rising one hundred-fifty to two hundred feet from where we were standing. Our spinning rods would almost throw a lure to the fish, but the fish were not interested in any kind of lure.

Watching those fish feed wildly and being unable to get close enough with our flies to get a strike left us disheartened. Just as the sun dropped below the mountain peak and the shade settled on the water the feeding fish spread out and moved closer to us, almost within our casting range.

I got down on my hands and knees and peered into the water. Moving around and between the rocks were very light-colored nymphs, probably a small tan colored species of the stonefly nymph which is very common in the high country. With great excitement I tied on a small Gold Rib Hares Ear, about the same body length as the nymphs that were moving around, and again started casting with my fly rod slowly working the nymph deep and between the rocks.

Suddenly I had a ferocious fish on the end of my line. Working it between the sharp rocks and boulders, somehow I landed it. I had caught a one and one-quarter pound cutthroat trout, my very first high mountain native cutthroat. A thrill that a flatlander will never forget and one of the most exciting times of my life. Two casts later, I had another strike and lost it in the rocks. Jim called to me, "Bob, its getting dark, we'd better get our rears out of here or we'll never find our way back to the Travelall."

He was right. By the time we reached the shore jumping from rock- to-rock in the semi-darkness, got our gear together and headed back, it was almost dark. The trip back was treacherous as one misstep and we could go rolling and tumbling down the steep, rocky slope or one wrong turn in the darkness of the trees and we would be lost in the alpine forest.

More by luck than knowledge we made our way back down the mountain in the dark. We carefully waded the stream which had now risen approximately two feet due to runoff caused by the melting snow during the heat of day. Tired, but happy, we arrived back home nearly fourteen hours after we had started our trip.

In reviewing the trip with Jim the following day, we found it quite depressing to have made a hard fourteen hour trip for probably twenty minutes of good fishing. Had we been able to reach out to the middle of the lake and presented a fly, we would have had at least an hour and a half of the best fishing of our lives.

This book describes thirty-seven years of study, equipment development, experiments and data gathering which would now turn that same trip into four hours of fun and exciting fishing.

The big change is due to the development of spinning equipment, the fillable plastic bubble and the fishing methods described in the following pages. We can now have all of the joy of fishing with a fly rod and still be able to easily reach fish one hundred to two hundred feet away.

This method has been proven to work in all still or slow moving water whether it be lake, reservoir, beaver pond or river. The method also works, with variations, on all fish that feed on insects or other aquatic life under the surface.

Chapter 1

Fishing the Fly-and-Bubble

The most important factor in successful fishing is . . . luck.
—Bob Kayne

Rocky Mountain anglers have developed this system of fishing the fly-and-bubble to enable them to cast up to two hundred feet or more and still have touch and accuracy in working their presentation. We wanted to be able to reach the fish and still have all of the excitement and pleasure of fighting the fish with a long, limber fly rod. The system evolved slowly as new materials, equipment, variations and ideas came forth from an untold number of avid fishermen. This method now gives the angler the opportunity to reach out to the fish and make a lifelike presentation of a fly or other bait in still water. You must get to where the fish are feeding to provoke a strike.

A. Questions and Answers

The most effective methods and optimum equipment are described in this book. But as a practical matter, if you were to ask the following questions you would get the following answers:
What rod can I use?

Answer: Any spinning or fly rod will work but a slow action fly rod, six foot or more in length with ceramic guides as described in Chapter 17 will give you better results. If you use a fly rod with the usual snake guides you will lose twenty-five to fifty feet of distance on your cast. With frequent fishing the snake guides will be worn down in about one season and need to be replaced. Replace the metal snake guides with ceramic guides. The rod will still work as a fly rod for normal fly fishing with the ceramic guides in place of the wire snake guides, but the ceramic guides give the added casting

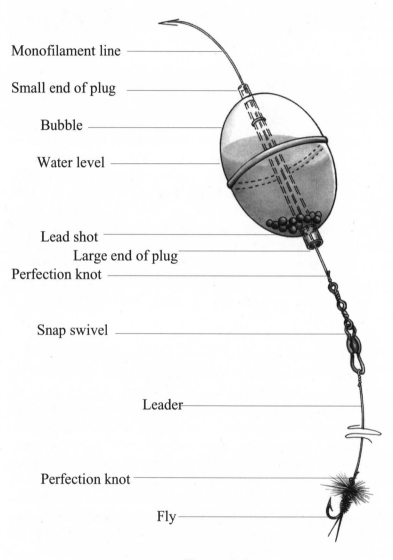

Monofilament line

Small end of plug

Bubble

Water level

Lead shot
Large end of plug
Perfection knot

Snap swivel

Leader

Perfection knot

Fly

Figure 1-1
Optimum Equipment Hookup

distance often needed to reach the fish and will last several seasons of hard fishing.

What reel should I use?

Answer: Any good quality spinning reel will work. A fly reel or bait casting reel will not give you the ability to cast long distances. An open faced spinning reel will allow you to cast the greatest distance.

What kind of line should I use?

Answer: Any good quality monofilament line or co-polymer line from four pound to twelve pound test. Six pound or eight pound test line is the optimum to give you maximum distance and sufficient tensile strength to land a large fish.

What fly should I use?

Answer: The fish may take any fly. Preferred patterns with variation to increase fly action in still water fishing are described in Chapter 5. In addition, you can also use this method with lures too small to be effectively cast one hundred fifty to two hundred feet with normal spinning equipment. This method can also be used with any manner of live bait as described in Chapter 13.

What kind of bubble should I use?

Answer: The fillable, clear, plastic bubble of 1 3/4 or 2 inch length will work in all circumstances.

How should this equipment be rigged?

Answer: See Figure 1-1, Optimum Equipment Hookup. The optimum hookup as shown in Figure 1-1 also needs a little explanation.

After threading the line through the rod guides, the line is then threaded through the center of the bubble plug. Thread the line through the small end of the bubble plug first. To reverse the threading through the bubble will cause pressure on the small end of the bubble plug when you cast and retrieve. That pressure will push the center plug out of the bubble causing the water to escape from the bubble and necessitate constant refilling of the bubble. By having the snap swivel pushing against the large opening of the center plug when you cast and retrieve, the swivel is pushing the bubble tight every cast. This keeps the plug firmly in place and prevents the water from escaping from the bubble.

What size snap swivel should I use?

Answer: Usually a #12 or #14 snap swivel will just enter the large hole end of the bubble's center plug. This is the best arrangement as it permits the bubble to also be used for fishing live bait (see Chapter 13). However anything that will stop the leader or line from sliding through the bubble plug will work, such as a swivel, split ring or even a piece of stick. Just remember, do not pinch the line or leader as any loss of diameter will cause the line or leader to lose its strength and break.

What knot should I use with monofilament or co-polymer lines?

Answer: The perfection knot and the Orvis knot are the only two knots that will give you maximum line strength. Most knots described in fly fishing books were designed for tying the old gut leaders, string, rope, and materials other than monofilament and co-polymer. Those knots are not suitable for monofilament or co-polymer lines. All other knots will cause pinching of the monofilament and co-polymer which causes those materials to lose most of it's strength.

B. Knots
1. The Orvis Knot.

The Orvis knot is amazing in that it will often provide a knot strength even greater than the stated line test strength. How is that possible? How can you get a seven pound knot strength out of a six pound test line?

The answer lies in the method of determining line strength. Line strength is determined by the breaking point of a one hundred foot length of line. The weakest point or smallest diameter in the one hundred foot length determines the line's pound test strength. This is the main reason why good quality lines can have a much smaller diameter than poor quality lines. The diameter of the good quality line is simply more consistent and has fewer weak spots.

When you use a piece of line for casting or for leader material a short piece of line is normally used. The strength of the short piece, unless it happens to contain the weakest section in a one hundred foot length, will be more then the stated test strength of the line. It was not uncommon in our testing of the Orvis knot for the line to break at a location other than the knot.

The Orvis knot is the more difficult knot to tie in bad light, with cold fingers or with the wind blowing. I only attempt it when tying knots in the comfort of my home. The Orvis Company has graciously provided the diagram shown in Fig. 1-2 and The Orvis Company has given permission to reproduce the information for your use.

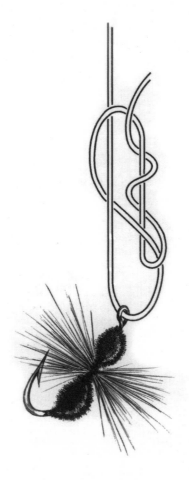

Figure 1-2
The Orvis Knot

Instructions for tying the Orvis Knot: Tippet to Fly

a. Thread tippet through eye of the hook.
b. Form a loop by bringing the tag end down behind the leader thus forming a loop.
c. Bring the tag end up and to the right behind itself and through the first loop and thus forming the second loop.
d. Rotate the tag end to the left and wrap twice through the second loop going behind each time.
e. Pull the fly with your right hand and the tag end and leader with your left hand until the knot tightens down slightly. Then let go of the tag end, moisten the knot and cinch it tight. Trim the tag end.

2. Perfection Knot.

The perfection knot is the easiest to tie of the two knots. When it is cold or the wind is blowing I use it exclusively. I discovered this knot in the 1960's when monofilament first became inexpensive and popular. I have only seen this knot illustrated once. Then it just disappeared from all of the literature. Could it be that it was too good and slowed line sales? Forget about all of the fancy fly-tying knots shown by fly fishermen in their books and manuals. All of those knots were designed for braided line or gut leader material. Braided line, gut leader and other materials do not rely on line diameter for their strength as do the monofilament and co-polymer lines. Remember any decrease in diameter of monofilament or co-polymer line decreases the line strength by the square root. Therefore an eight pound test monofilament line that is pinched to one-half of it's diameter has only 2.83 pounds of strength not four pounds strength as most people would think.

The perfection knot will give you approximately 95 percent line strength when properly tied. Only the Orvis knot will do as well or even better. If not properly tied, the line will be pinched and the line will easily break when you attempt to cinch up the knot.

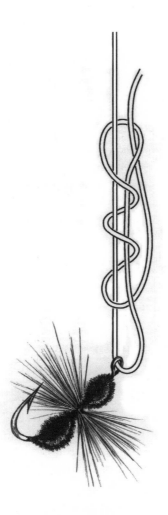

Figure 1-3
Perfection Knot

Figure 1-3 illustrates the tying of the perfection knot. It is recommended that you practice this knot at home before you go out to fish. You should be able to tie this knot in the dark with your fingers numb and stiff from the cold and without any concentration or thought on your part. It is not efficient to waste good fishing time trying to tie a new knot on your line when you should have your line in the water and be fishing.

Tying the Perfection Knot

1. Pass the leader through the eye of the hook giving approximately six inches of leader with which to work.
2. Bring the leader end up the line two to three inches and hold both lines together with your fingers. (Hint) gently stick the point of the hook into the side of your hand or use one of a variety of hook holders to keep the hook stable and in place.
3. Continue holding the two lines together with your fingers. A loop will form when the line is now turned down toward the hook for winding.
4. Wind the leader down both lines toward the hook - use five turns.
5. Pass the end of the leader through the loop formed just above the eye of the hook.
6. Bring the end of the leader up the line and now pass it through the loop formed by the line being held by your fingers.
7. Wet the knot with saliva to make the line slide freely.
8. Gently pull the leader so as to slip the five turns of the line down to the eye of the hook.
9. Gently pull the end of the leader to tighten and set the knot.
10. Holding the hook with your fingers, firmly pull the leader against the hook to test its strength. If not tied correctly the line will easily break. If the line breaks try again.
11. Trim off the excess line.

C. Snap Swivels

The snap swivel should be of good quality. A ball bearing snap swivel is highly recommended. For many uses it is an advantage to have a swivel whose top loop is small enough to just fit into the large end of the bubble's center plug. The top loop of most ball bearing swivels is too large to slip inside of the center plug and therefore may not be practical when this feature is needed.

Snap swivels in sizes number 12 and 14 will usually have a loop that will just fit into the large end of the center of the bubble plug. Keep some of both sizes in your tackle box or fly vest. When rigging up your gear, pick out the size that enters into the large end of that particular bubble plug and stays in place. Do not use a swivel so small that it completely enters the bubble plug. A swivel small enough to move completely up into the bubble plug can easily get stuck making it impossible to remove the swivel when you need to tie on a new leader or broken line.

D. Leaders

Always use leader material at least two pounds lighter than your line. This provides for the loss of only a leader and your fly or bait when you are snagged. In the case of a snag or any other obstruction, the bubble is not lost. A one hundred foot spool of monofilament line, two pounds lighter test than your casting line will provide you with plenty of good leader material at a nominal price. Under most fishing conditions, four pound test line is adequate for your leader material. In some instances six pound test line may have some advantages such as when you are putting your lure through weeds or rocky areas that may snag or weaken the leader.

When fishing with a fly, try to keep the length of the leader the same as the length of your rod or a little longer. If you can effectively cast the longer leader without difficulty, the longer leader can sometimes increase the number of strikes. When sitting in a boat a leader six inches to one foot shorter that your rod makes casting easier as the shorter leader may keep the fly from touching the water on the back cast. Never, never stand in a small boat when casting.

For fishing lures a short leader is easier to cast. The weight of the lure at the end of a long leader makes a long leader inefficient. Use a leader only long enough so as not to impede the action of the lure.

When fishing bait, the length of the leader is determined by the depth you wish your bait to reach.

If fishing for game fish that have sharp teeth, use a wire leader or spider line for the full length of the leader or just the last six inches to one foot as you prefer. Here a simple barrel knot can be used to connect the two line together.

Chapter 2

Bubbles

The first use of plastic bubbles of which I have knowledge were the large six inch long solid plastic bubbles used on the Pacific coast for ocean fishing. These bubbles allowed us to cast live bait with our spooled reels. The first small bubbles for fresh water fishing were developed in about 1957 and were the torpedo-style solid bubbles with a metal eye screwed into each end. The line and leader were tied to the eyes.

The torpedo-style bubble was the first bubble used in the Rocky Mountains. This bubble would finally permit a long cast of a fly or light lure with standard spinning equipment. The torpedo shaped bubbles came in only one weight and they floated. This bubble was effective as long as the fish were near the surface and the weight was proper for your equipment. The torpedo bubble is still used occasionally and are quite effective for night fishing. They will refract moonlight which can create very exciting fishing opportunities.

One hot August evening in 1959, a group of us packed into Long Lake in Colorado's Roosevelt National Forest to fish for brown trout at night. Long Lake contained many browns from five to nine pounds, but very seldom did anyone ever see one of those trophy fish during the daylight hours.

We had heard stories that some of these large browns had been caught after dark. The fly tiers in the group created large night flies constructed of white and black Guinea Hen hackles. These thick bodied flies we believed would be visible when the fish were looking up against a moonlit sky. The Guinea hackle flies were attached using the knots as shown in the previous chapter. They were then cast from shore as far as possible with our spinning outfits and slowly trolled back to the shore.

The moonlight was on the water and the night was clear and crisp. Jim was lazily bringing in his fly-and-bubble when the water exploded below his bubble throwing the bubble two feet into the air. Although the night was bright, the water looked black and foreboding. Long Lake is often referred to as a bottomless lake. Although I'm certain it is not bottomless, I know it is at least one hundred fifty feet deep. The thought of a fish that big in a lake that deep put a chill through our spines as we had often waded out up to our chests to fish the lake during the daylight hours.

About the time we all calmed down from the shock of the strike, Caroll's bubble also exploded from the water. Suddenly, and at the same time, we all realized what had happened. Those huge browns were attacking the bubbles which were easily seen as they refracted the moonlight and moved along the surface of the lake.

In a complete panic we quickly hauled in our lines and started digging through our equipment to find a way to attach hooks to the torpedo bubbles. In an effort to reduce weight, because of the mile and a half uphill hike at high altitude, we had cut our gear to the bare necessities. We had to carry in food, water, rain gear, heavy coats, hip boots, lanterns, flashlights, and our fishing gear. Not one of us had a treble hook or even a single hook larger than size 8.

We huddled around the campfire trying to tie on our small hooks with pieces of leader material to the eyes of the torpedo bubble. The first one out promptly hooked onto a very large fish, and the fish had no problem breaking the three pound test leader and making off with his little hook. Six or eight lost fish later, we decided to call it a night and just go home empty handed. We were simply not prepared to handle an infuriated eight pound brown trout on a number 8 hook with a three pound test leader.

The floating bubble usually does not provide good fishing as it keeps the fly near the surface. Most of the time the fish are near the bottom of the lake or in the weed beds.

Years later the fillable bubble appeared in our sporting goods stores, and this design of bubble meets all of our fishing needs.

The fillable bubble is approximately two inches long and has a tapered tube used as a plug down the center of the bubble. By pushing the small end of the tapered tube, the plug will pop out and the bubble can be pushed under the water to fill it with the amount of water you desire.

The amount of water you put into the bubble will depend upon the weight needed to cast, and whether you want the bubble to float or sink. See Figure 1-1. A larger bubble of the same design is also being marketed and has practical uses when additional weight is needed or more buoyancy for larger live baits is required.

The fillable bubble is easily broken, so at least six bubbles should be in your tackle box or fishing vest. Save the cracked bubbles as they are easily repaired with model airplane glue or clear fingernail polish.

The question is often asked: "Why not just use lead weight to get the casting distance you need?" The answer lies in the lack of control in fishing a lead weight. It would take four ounces of lead to attain the casting distance of a water filled bubble.

The lead weight being much heavier than water quickly sinks to the bottom and constantly pulls the line and fly down into the mud or weeds. The plastic bubble provides the weight necessary for a long cast but weights little when below the surface of the water. This is because the bubble is filled with water which is weightless under water. Once the bubble is under water the only weight on the line is the weight of the plastic and any lead shot placed in the bubble. Even this weight is offset by the weight of the water the plastic and lead displaces. The plastic bubble provides the weight needed for long casts and the buoyancy required for delicate fishing.

(See page 161 for fly-and-bubble supplies.)

Figure 2-1
Adult Mayfly

Chapter 3

Rods, Reels. Lines and Hooks

Although as previously stated almost any rod, spinning reel and monofilament line will work in fly-and-bubble fishing. The purpose of using this fishing method is to get the maximum distance with your cast and to get the fly down below the surface of the water where the fish are suspended. This is especially necessary when fishing from shore on small bodies of still water where the fish tend to feed or lay out of normal casting distance. However, this method is also efficient when fishing from a boat and the fish start rising or working one hundred feet or more from the boat and you wish to cast to them instead of moving the boat closer to the rises and risk spooking the fish.

A. Rods

Pleasure is the name of the game when fishing. The more fish you catch the greater your fishing pleasure. The more sensitive your rod, the greater your pleasure when fighting and landing the fish. The greatest pleasure is felt when hooking, fighting and landing a fish on a long sensitive fly rod. Even a small fish can give a good battle on the right equipment. A large, strong fish provides the opportunity to test your skills. There is nothing like the excitement of fishing with a fly rod. This method of fishing is perfect for the use of a fly rod.

The primary element in obtaining maximum distance in fly-and-bubble fishing is the rod. The important factors are balance, action and length. When those three factors are coordinated casting is effortless and a thing of beauty. The perfect rod for this style of fishing is a slow action fiberglass fly rod eight to nine feet in length and rebuilt using ceramic guides.

Any slow action fly rod will work, but most other rod materials are much more expensive and do not have any advantages over the fiber glass rod. The slow action permits accelerating the speed of the bubble without snap which could break the line. The fly rod handle places the spinning reel behind your hand. With the length of the rod and the weight of the bubble it is possible to have the balance point of the rod in the palm of your hand.

Balancing the rod in the palm of your hand eases the strain on the wrist and the carpel tunnel. It permits casting for long periods of time reducing pain or fatigue in your hand and wrist. You can start fly-and-bubble fishing effectively with any fly rod, but for maximum results build a rod for this specific purpose. Building a custom rod for fly-and-bubble fishing is a wonderful project for those long winter months when you can't fish but still have day dreams of the fishing season to come.

The delicate action of a fly rod is one of the fundamental reasons sportsmen love to fly fish. The fly rod can still be used for normal fly fishing even after it has been rebuilt with ceramic guides. If you wish to change from fly-and-bubble fishing to normal fly fishing just carry a fly fishing reel and mount it for fly fishing whenever the urge or conditions make fly fishing more desirable.

By the end of one fishing season you will notice that the fly rod snake guides are getting worn. The fast moving monofilament line passing through the snake guides quickly grinds down the snake guides. Fly rod snake guides are not designed to take this wear. At this point the snake guides will have to be replaced. This makes it the ideal time to replace the metal snake guides with ceramic spinning guides.

The ceramic guides will increase the casting distance by decreasing friction of the line going through the guides. The ceramic guides will not noticeably effect the action of the fly rod for normal fly fishing. In fact the ceramic guides will increase your ability to shoot fly line while fly fishing using the same rod. Chapter 17 describes the steps to build or rebuild a fly rod for fly-and-bubble fishing.

B. Reels

Any good quality spinning reel will be efficient for this method of fishing. Some people prefer the closed-faced reel for easier handling and freedom from the birds nest and tangles that are a problem on windy days with open faced reels. Remember, the main purpose of the fly-and-bubble system is to get maximum distance. For maximum distance a good quality open faced reel is needed. With the open faced reel you will have to cope with the normal problems of wind throwing off loops and an occasional "bird's nest" as happens when using small diameter line. This is a small price to pay for the extra twenty to fifty feet you can attain by using an open-faced reel.

Because you will be fishing with your line on your finger as described in Chapter 8, Section G, it is best to have a reel that rotates the line toward your open index finger. A reel that turns in the opposite direction will bring the line to the back of your hand and finger and make it difficult to catch the line and keep the line in the proper position.

C. Lines

Always keep in mind that you must reach the fish to catch them. If the fish are out of casting range you will not be successful. The main object of your equipment is to get the greatest casting distance. That will allow you to reach more fish. The best rod and reel will not accomplish maximum distance if the line is too heavy or the reel spool is not full. To attain the maximum casting distance the smallest practical diameter line should be used. In good quality monofilament lines six pound test seems to be optimum. With the new co-polymer line you can easily go to eight pound test and still reach the maximum casting distance with the least amount of thrown loops and tangles. Use a good quality line of one to two pound lower test for your leader material.

Always keep the spool of the reel full of line. A reel spool with a low line level will cause the line to rub against the spool causing friction and decrease the casting distance.

D. Hooks.

1. Fly Hooks.

In Chapter 5. Flies the patterns suggest the proper hook size and style for each fly. Note that most flies are tied on long shank hooks rather then the "regular" length hooks used in most dry fly patterns. The shank of the hook is the straight portion of the hook extending from immediately behind the eye to the beginning of the bend, i.e. the curved portion of the hook. Although there is no standard relationship between length of shank, bend and gape (the distance between the point and the shank) among the different manufacturers and styles of hooks, the actual differences are so small as to be inconsequential.

Most patterns described use a long shank hook denoted as 1XL, 2XL, 3XL, etc. This means that the hook has a longer shank than the regular hook of that size. The differences are small but important to that pattern. Using a size 8 hook as an illustration, the regular hook shank length is 11/16 of an inch, the 1XL is 1/16th of an inch longer or 3/4 of an inch long, the 2XL is another 1/16th of an inch longer or 13/16 of an inch long and so on. the same proportions hold true for other sizes of hooks.

2. Bait hooks.

In bait fishing use the size and style of hook you are most comfortable with. My personal preference is a short shank hook with just enough gape and bend to closely cover the bait. The short shank hooks are designated as 1XS, 2XS, 3XS and so on, just like the long hooks except with each additional X the shank is getting shorter than the regular size hook. I personally like the bait hook platted in gold. The gold seems to give a little flash which the fish can see from a long distance. This I believe will attract the fish to the bait.

Chapter 4

Understanding Fish Psychology and Physiology

A. Fish Don't Think!

Forget what you have read in all of the fly fishing articles, books and tales. FISH CANNOT THINK! All scientific studies show conclusively that fish do not have any ability to think, to reason, or to make conscious decisions. Their brain system is genetically and environmentally programmed and they can only react to appropriate stimuli.

Although scientists do not understand the mechanism of the programming of the fish brain any more than they can understand the mechanism of the programming of a human brain, they have conclusively proved that fish are genetically and environmentally programmed to act without conscious thought as we perceive thought.

Fish can learn or be programmed by the environment if they are lucky enough to survive the experience. Fish do not reason or think, but only respond to certain stimuli. The secret of catching fish is not to outsmart them, but simply not to trigger their defense mechanisms and instead to trigger their strike mechanism.

When you see a fish following your lure but not strike, it is because the fish has been stimulated to follow or chase the lure by the lure's movement, but the striking mechanism has not been triggered. The fish has not in any measure reasoned that something looks wrong with the lure or that the lure doesn't act right. It simply has not had its striking mechanism triggered.

How do you trigger a fish's striking mechanism? That depends somewhat on the species of fish. Each species has evolved differently and has distinct genetic programming. Fish such as catfish are genetically programmed to feed primarily by the use of scent. Other fish, such as trout, are genetically programmed to strike by sight and movement. Therefore, it is unlikely to catch a catfish on a lure or fly unless those catfish have been environmentally reprogrammed to survive by taking food that moves.

All fish are non-specific opportunists when it comes to eating. Some trout have been environmentally programmed to feed by scent in order to survive and some catfish have been environmentally programmed to feed by sight and movement in order to survive. If fishing for catfish with a fly you had better impregnate the fly with catfish scent or your chances of triggering a strike become very slim. On the other hand if fishing for trout or panfish with a fly, fish it with an action and at the appropriate location where the fly's movement will trigger a strike by the fish.

Normally, in fishing a fly-and-bubble, do not fish on the surface of the water. However, I must admit that it is very exciting to throw out the first cast with a fly-and-bubble, have the fly lay on the surface for a few seconds and watch a fish rise up to the surface and suck it in. This can and does happen. Fish do not often feed on the surface, but rather habitually feed just below the surface on the nymphs as they struggle to reach the surface of the water, or as the nymphs or other aquatic life swim from one spot to another. The fish feed below the surface because that is where the food is 99 per cent of the time.

Take a set of field glasses and closely watch the surface of the water the next time you see fish rising on the lake. You will discover that it is not often that the head of the fish is disturbing the water, but rather it is the dorsal fin or tail fin, which is breaking the surface. Often no part of the fish is actually breaking the surface. The movement of the fish just below the surface of the water has created a swirl. This is because the fish are swimming below the surface of the water and taking nymphs as they approach the surface. Sometime the fish dive to catch the insect when it appears below them in their line of sight causing the fish's tail to break the water's surface as the fish literally stands on its head.

Therefore, when fishing a fly-and-bubble for fish that you see rising or disturbing the surface, your fly should be six inches to three feet below the surface as that is where the fish are programmed to look for food.

Any wet fly pattern may trigger a fish into striking. Experience has taught that some wet fly patterns or variations of wet fly patterns seem to be more effective in the fly-and-bubble style of fishing. When fishing lakes or other still water with the fly-and-bubble, imitate the food sources in that body of water. In the Midwest and Eastern United States that would mean some kind of imitation of the mayfly nymph or hellgrammite. Other flies that imitate food items as a leech would be a black Woolly Bugger. A food item such as a minnow, imitated by the Hornberg, is a good producer.

In the Rocky Mountains and in the Western United States where the predominant aquatic fish food is the damsel fly nymph and the stone fly nymph, the fly patterns would be different.

If you tie your own flies, use a wet fly hook with a turned down eye. The heavier hook helps the fly to sink and the turned down eye, when fished properly, will give the fly a little extra wiggle or action. When selecting a fly pattern for the first cast, consider each of the four S's, size, shade, silhouette and scent. Do so methodically to cover the following variations of size, color and pattern.

Size

By size we really mean length of the fly. You want the fly length to be consistent with the size of the aquatic life in that particular body of water on which the fish normally feed. The patterns described below list hook sizes that should match the size of the aquatic life it was designed to represent. The hook size can be increased or decreased to meet the requirements of the aquatic life in the body of water you are fishing.

Shade

Note the word "color" was not used. Current scientific opinion theorizes that fish cannot detect color. At least not as humans see color. Now none of these scientists can get into the brain of a fish any more than they can get into the brain of a human. There is no method that can prove humans actually perceive the same sensation when looking at the same color. For all we know two people looking at the color you have been trained to call red may actually see yellow or green if looking through the other's eyes. All may call the color red, but in your mind you actually see something completely different.

Prevailing theory is that fish are what humans call "color blind" and see everything in shades of gray. Assuming that this theory is correct, is color important or should all lures just be prepared in shades of gray? Well it may be red to us and gray to the fish, but all experienced fishermen know at times that the shade of gray produced by the color red sets off the striking mechanism and catches fish when no other color (or shade of gray produced by that red) will provoke a strike. The best policy is to use color but be aware of shade. Don't use black when the food supply is light green.

Silhouette

The outline of the fly as seen from the side or below is very important. If the fish are feeding on a thin bodied nymph such as the mayfly and you are fishing a thick bodied fly your chances of triggering the striking mechanism diminish. The great success of the Royal Coachman fly is probably due more to its unique shape than to any other factor. The Royal Coachman is pretty enough to catch both fish and fisherman. That is what makes it such a great fly pattern. Fishermen are attracted to it and so are the fish. Make sure that the fly you are using at least matches the aquatic life of the lake by being thin or thick.

Scent

The odor the fly emits is not usually of much importance. One of the exceptions is described in Chapter 11, Section E, Catfish. Many good and experienced fisherman firmly believe that scent is the most important factor in their fishing success no matter what the fish species. Having seen some of their successes I certainly would not argue that they are wrong. Whether you chose to use a homemade or commercial scent there is no reason to believe that it can do any harm. However, be cautious when using insect repellent. It is only logical that a scent that would repel insects, the main food of most fish, would also repel fish.

One of the best ways to decide what fly to select is to examine the shallow water along the shore of the lake. You can do this by simply getting into the water and slowly roll over any log that is always submerged or partly submerged. You will eventually find nymphs and other insects clinging to the underside of a log. They tend to release themselves from the log as it is rolled, but if you watch the water closely you can see the nymphs swimming away and that gives information as to size, color and shape of the insects on which the fish in that lake feed.

Be sure to always turn the log back to its original position and location. Leave it the way you found it, as a great deal of the lake's food chain is on that log and not visible. The food chain in the lake can often be harmed by exposing it to the light.

You can also examine a lake by slowly turning over submerged rocks along the shore of the lake. The rocks should be at least the size of a softball and should be moved very slowly so as not to raise any dirt that would hide the insects. Again always return the rock to its original position to preserve the aquatic food chain in the body of water.

The best way to investigate the food chain in the lake is by using a long handled minnow net. I purchased a rubber netted long handled bass net, removed the rubber net, and replaced it with a 30 inch minnow net. With this net, I can dig into the nearest weed bed and by dragging the minnow net through the weed bed and along the bottom, quickly collect specimens of the most prominent fish food in the lake. Examining the contents of the minnow net often gives the information needed to determine the size, color, and thickness of the fly you should use in that lake.

Wherever I use the minnow net to examine the water for aquatic life, my fishing success goes up dramatically. By the use of the sample net I have probably discovered more about that lake in ten minutes than most people who have fished there for many years.

On one long weekend many summers ago my young son and I were fishing Diamond Lake in Wyoming. I used the minnow net to sweep through the weed bed along the shore, and came up with three salamanders, or what are commonly called waterdogs. People we met at the lake who had been fishing there for years had no idea that the lake contained salamanders.

We were camped there to fly fish and did not have adequate tackle to utilize the salamanders. An attempt was made to construct a harness of no. 6 hooks and leader material. We did have a trolled six inch salamander actually bitten in half by the trout in that lake but we were unable to hook one of those big lunkers with our inadequate rigs. It was a thrill to feel the strikes, but it would have been much more exciting had we been able to land one of those large trout.

Using the sample net will always provide valuable information even if it comes up empty. An empty net would tell you there is little or no food in the lake. No food means small starving fish.

B. Weather Conditions and Other Factors

If you have spent any time reading fishing books or outdoor sports magazines you will have already been exposed to untold articles and theories of when it is best to catch fish. Some authors swear by lunar cycles and Solar Tables, others use barometric pressure, weather fronts, direction of the wind, water temperature, time of day, fishing before or after or even during a rain, biorhythms and the amount of pain in the author's knee due to an old football injury. Do any of these fishing indicators work? Of course they do. At least they do for that particular author who believes in them. Do any of these authors catch fish during these particular conditions? Of course they do.

When a reasonably good fisherman decides he is going fishing just before a cold front blows into the area he will catch fish. Is it due to the change of conditions caused by the arrival of the cold front? Maybe, but more likely it's because that's when he went fishing. I can absolutely and unequivocally guarantee that he did not catch any fish sitting in the living room waiting for the cold front to arrive.

Some writers are so intent on their pet theories that there have even been poems written concerning their beliefs. One such poem, as I remember it, concerns the direction of the wind and goes something like this:

When the wind comes from the east, That's the time the fish do feast.

When the wind comes from the west, That's the time the fish the fish bite best.

When the wind comes from the south, It blows the bait into the fish's mouth.

But when the wind comes from the north, That's the time to head to port.

Those of you who fish frequently will probably think of times when the wind was blowing from the east, west and south and this little limerick was very accurate. But if you have fished enough you know that there are many times when the wind blows from the north that the fishing was also absolutely sensational.

The real rule to catching fish is that to catch fish you must go fishing and be a good enough fisherman to adjust to the conditions existing at that time.

A good example of this happened on October 31 when a friend and I went fishing at one of my favorite spots, Red Feather Lakes in Colorado. It had already been a cold fall and this day the wind was sharp, cold and coming in from the north. We had spent most of the afternoon fishing several of my favorite hot spots on the lake with little success. The only strikes we had were close to the shore, sometimes the fish struck just as we were lifting the fly from the water.

My fingers were freezing. My feet were freezing and I was about to give it up for the day. After all, the wind was right out of the north and sometimes it contained icy snow flakes. One last try and then head down the mountain and go home. I stepped out on a point. To the right was a shallow bay area. Probably one to three feet deep as far out as I could cast. To the left of the point the depth dropped off and that is where I could usually catch some fish. I was using the side arm cast as I was trying to keep my bubble under the north wind blowing into my face. Fingers stiff with the cold, the cast went to the right into the shallow water bay that was usually full of weeds and where I had never caught a fish. "Damn," I muttered, "better get it out of there quick. No, the rule is to fish every cast just as if it is a good cast." I'm sure you have guessed the result. The two and one half pound, hook jawed, dark colored, buck rainbow trout had the reel screaming as the monofilament line sang in the wind.

It seemed that all the big fish in the lake had gathered in the shallow bay where the water was the warmest and those big lunkers were just laying there waiting for something to feed on. Over the next two hours we had some of the best fishing of the year as the north wind blew snow into our faces and all the cold and numbness amazingly disappeared. I can now hardly wait until the same conditions arise and see if the fish are laying in that shallow water again.

Remembering that the fish are only interested in two things: *eating* and *reproduction*. Use that knowledge to increase your success while fishing. Always remember that fish are simple cold-blooded animals that do not make automobiles, write books, build homes, or engage in any activities other than feeding and reproducing.

One factor which has been scientifically measured through various studies is the effect of water temperature on the energy level of fish. Those who are familiar with the outdoors have seen the effect of temperature on other cold-blooded animals such as snakes and lizards. Personal observations make it obvious that cold-blooded animals have a different level of activity or metabolism at different temperatures.

The fish being a cold-blooded animal, its metabolism is also affected by water temperature. Many scientific studies have been conducted concerning the temperature factor, and although they do not agree exactly, their general conclusions are in accord. Water temperature does effect the movement and feeding requirements of the fish.

The following chart indicates the optimum water temperature for the stated species of fish. Studies may vary one or two degrees in either direction, but for our purposes that would make no significant difference. At the temperatures stated the fish are the most active and are on the move hunting for food. As the water temperature moves away from those optimum temperatures in either direction, the fish tend to become less active, burn up less energy and need less food. This leads to the conclusion that as the water temperature moves toward the optimum temperature, the fish become more and more active and feed more aggressively. A good fisherman uses this knowledge to locate fish and also catch more fish.

Perch: 63°F
Bluegills: 78°F
Brook Trout: 62°F
Brown Trout: 70°F
Largemouth Bass: 71°F
Muskellunge: 55°F
Pike: 67°F
Rainbow Trout: 65°F
Smallmouth Bass: 67°F
Walleyes: 64°F

Some understanding of the physical qualities of water can also aid the fisherman in determining where to locate his quarry. The specific gravity, or heaviness of water is greatest at 39°F. Above that temperature water is lighter. Much below that temperature, water turns to ice to become lighter still and floats on the surface.

Understanding the physics of water allows you to determine where the fish are most likely to find the greatest comfort zone at the optimum temperature stated in the list above.

From late Fall to early Spring, the water at the bottom of the lake should be 39°F. If there is deep ice in a shallow lake the deepest spot in the lake may well be the warmest place in the lake at 39°F. Fish will tend to seek that comfortable temperature, and stay at the very bottom of the deepest portion of the lake.

Water flowing into the lake from snow and ice runoff in early spring would be entering the lake at approximately 32°F to 40°F. Although the spring runoff will also bring food into the lake, the fish may find the low temperature uncomfortable and seek out warmer areas of the lake in which to feed or suspend.

Fish also tend to lie in wait next to the cold current of water flowing into the lake at the inlet. The fish will lay in the adjacent warmer water waiting for food to flow by. They tend to maintain a position as much out of the cold current as possible so that the fish can dart into the current, take the food going by and then return to its feeding station in the warmer water.

Underground spring water may enter the lake with a temperature from 45°F to boiling, as in the case of hot springs. Generally underground springs will enter the lake at the approximate temperature of the crust of the earth which is about 58°F. Knowing this it is easy to reason that the fish will seek out the underground spring when the lake water is 75°F and above the fish's comfort zone or the fish will move into the spring water when the adjacent water is below the fish's comfort zone. Using the various factors already brought forth in this book, analyzing where and when to fish a particular lake as illustrated in the following scenario:

Scenario - Spring, heavy snow and ice runoff, sunny day.

Analysis - The runoff would bring a large quantity of food into the lake at the inlet. The supply of food would normally attract fish to the flowing water. In addition, fish are programmed to move to running water and would gravitate to the inlet of the lake. However, because of the low temperature of the water entering the lake would be below the fish's comfort zone, the fish will not get directly into the cold flow at the inlet. The fish will probably lay off to the side of the flowing water where the water has already been warmed by the sun. The fish would then dart into the colder water to grab morsels of food and immediately return to the warmer water. Casting just to the side of the fast current should put your offering right in front of the fish.

Later in the afternoon when the water in the shallows is warm and in the shade, the fish would gravitate to the warmer, shallow water to feed on insects. The fish would only move to the shallow water at sunset. After the sun was off the water the fish is not subject to attack from above.

C Strike Zone

Fish, like humans, have three basic senses: 1. sight, 2. hearing and 3. smell.

1. Sight

The eyesight of fish is much like that of humans. The zone of sight or "strike zone" is a cone shaped area. It is almost perpendicular to the sides or peripherally. Above the fish's head it is also almost perpendicular. There is little vision below the fish and none behind the fish. It is important that your offering be placed within that cone shaped strike zone of the fish. Normally, a fish will not strike something it cannot see.

2. Hearing

The hearing mechanism of the fish is much different than a humans. The fish is living in a liquid (water) rather than a gas (air). Sound travels much stronger and further in a liquid than a gas. Sound or vibration is perceived by the force caused by molecules bouncing off each other. The molecules are closer together in a liquid than a gas. The shorter distance traveled between the molecules results in faster contact and faster transmission of sound. The sound is also much sharper as the particles simply do not lose as much velocity traveling the shorter distance between molecules in a liquid. If you have ever played pocket pool or billiards, you see the same principal in effect with every shot. When aiming at a ball across the table it takes time for the cue ball to get there and the cue ball loses speed before it reaches the target. If aiming at a ball close to the cue ball with the same stroke, the strike is quick and the impact hard.

Studies have shown that whales can hear the calls of other whales over a hundred miles away. Fish do not have ears but rather have sensors located along the lateral line on each side of the body. These sensors are very sensitive to any vibration in the water. This is not of much help to the fisherman using flies, but is important to the fisherman using plugs or live bait such as minnows. The vibrations of the plug or minnow will cause the fish to turn its body to put the cause of the vibration in the strike zone. It is probable that the riffle created by the bubble when moving along the surface can be sensed by the fish and cause the fish to turn or move its body to place the cause of the vibration into the strike zone.

3. Smell

The olfactory system of the fish is much like that of humans in that the fish can sense minute particles of a substance in the water just as other animals sense minute particles in the air. This sense is more highly developed in fish than it is in humans. Most of the animal kingdom has a highly developed sense of smell when compared to man. Because the molecules in a liquid are closer together than molecules in a gas, the particles travel much slower in the liquid. As the travel time for the particles in a liquid is very long, scents are usually of little use to the fly fisherman.

Chapter 5

Flies

Most of those beautiful, colorful flies you see in the sporting goods stores were designed to catch fisherman, not fish. In addition those few patterns that were designed to catch fish were designed for fishing moving water, such as a stream or river, either above or below the surface.

If the fly is riding on the surface of the water then the current makes the fly look like other insects riding on the surface. In the event the fly is below the surface, the varying pressures caused by the moving water cause the feathers and other materials to vibrate and move so as to make the fly look alive and lifelike.

This is not the situation when fishing placid waters such as a large pool, pond or lake. To make the fly look alive under these conditions, the fly must be altered and tied with slightly different materials and fished in the manner described in Chapters 8 and 9.

Tying flies for fly-and-bubble fishing does not require the expensive stiff-hackled feathers of the dry fly fisherman. Here you would rather use a lower grade, softer, and much less expensive hackle. In addition, you also use soft furs and a lot of marabou. Heavier hooks are desirable as they provide a little more weight to the fly and help the fly to remain under the surface where the fish are. Quite often a longer shank hook is indicated in the list of materials. In tight line fishing the fish tends to take the fly into its mouth and then turn. A hook with a smaller gape will still hook the fish under these conditions.

The symmetrical, neatly tied fly is also at a disadvantage in fly-and-bubble fishing. In fact, a fly that looks sloppily tied and not symmetrical has a large advantage. In working the fly through the water as described in Chapter 8, the non-symmetrical fly will tend to twist or move from side to side. This gives the impression of a live or injured insect or minnow. This is more likely to trigger a strike response from a waiting fish.

A fisherman I met on a lake several years ago handed me a glob of fur and feathers which he referred to as his "killer fly." He said that he tied them himself, and that they were real fish getters. He was also fishing with a fly-and-bubble. I took a scornful glance at the fly as it looked shabby and shapeless, but not wishing to offend a fellow fisherman I smiled and thanked him for the fly. The fly was stuck on my foam hat band thinking that some day in a desperate situation I might actually try it. The fly was a brownish, streamer type fly that looked like nothing more than a long glob of fur and hair.

A couple of years later, when I wasn't catching any fish, I searched my hat and spotted this "killer fly." Laughing to myself, I tied the brown glob to my leader, thinking that nothing else had really worked in the last half hour so I might as well try something this ridiculous.

Before tossing this shapeless thing into the lake I ran it through the water in front of me, and the darn thing actually wiggled. It looked like a little brown minnow wiggling along. Being an excitable and curious person, I immediately cast the fly next to a large rock sticking out of the lake. I knew that a large fish usually claimed its territory at the base of each side of that rock.

As the bubble approached the rock I swung the rod out to make sure the bubble did not hang up on the side of the boulder, but much to my surprise it did hang up. Probably the biggest darn fish in the lake grabbed that fly and I couldn't move it. The first twist of the fish's head broke loose the fly from the three pound test leader. To this day I wish that I had taken a better look at that fly. I would love to know how it was tied to make it wiggle in such an enticing manner.

I have racked my brain trying to remember just who the heck gave me that fly so I could contact him again. The wiggling action of that fly moving through the water made it a "killer fly" indeed.

Although at different times any fly pattern may catch fish, the following patterns, with the variations noted, appear to be the most potent and consistent producers for fly-and-bubble fishing.

Figure 5-1
Mayfly Nymph

A. Little Green Fly

This is the simplest fly to tie and probably the best producer of strikes. Over several years of experimenting, my youngest son and I developed this fly through many variations. The one described below seems to be the most productive. I am not certain what it is supposed to represent, but my guess would be it triggers the feeding response of a fish that feeds on damsel fly nymphs, mayfly nymphs, or other long skinny aquatic insects in their underwater stages. This fly should be fished very slowly and erratically in eight inch to one foot movements. The last stage of development of this fly was the use of goose biots for the tail. Looking at the nymph illustrations in this book demonstrate why the distinct two-pointed tail is such a great improvement.

Little Green Fly

Hook: #12 or #14, 2XL, turned down eye Mustad 9671 or 9672
Tail: 2 or 3 goose biots, green or olive.
Body: One layer of Peacock herl.
Hackle: Short, green or olive.

Figure 5-2
Little Green Fly

B. Woolly Bugger

If I were stranded in the wilderness and my survival rested on just one fly, I would pray that there would be a black Woolly Bugger in my fly box. Fished in quiet water it may represent a leech, small waterdog, or crawdad. Whatever it represents triggers the striking reaction of the fish and that is all that counts. The Woolly Bugger should be fished slowly with erratic action, a stop and go movement, to mimic the movement of a leech or crawdad. Over the years, I have noted that when fishing was slow and I caught a fish on a Woolly Bugger, that the fish had been feeding on crawdads. Whenever you're at a lake that you know contains crawdads and there is nothing working near the surface, a Woolly Bugger is a good first choice.

Woolly Bugger
    Hook: #8, 2XL or 3XL, turned down eye, Mustad 9671, 9672, or 73580.
    Tail: Black marabou, very full with six or eight strands of flash.
    Body: Medium black chenille.
    Hackle: Black tied Palmer over body.

Figure 5-3
Woolly Bugger

C. Hornberg

The hornberg pattern is a good representation of many of the small minnows which inhabit lakes and ponds. To make it act like a minnow in the water, it should be fished in short spurts of movement and stops. Observations of normal minnow action in the water show that minnows usually swim for a short distance in spurts and then stop and spurt again.

Hornberg

Hook: #6 or #8, 1XL turned down eye Mustad 3906, 3906B
   or 79570B.
Tail: None.
Body: Silver tinsel.
Wing: Yellow marabou.
Sides: Barred woodcock, tips glued together.

D. Marabou Adams

The Adams pattern has been triggering fish to strike for decades. By modifying it with a soft hackle and either soft white feather or marabou as wings makes it a very satisfactory fly for fly-and-bubble fishing. It should be worked slowly and erratically in eight inch to one foot movements

Maribou Adams

Hook: #12 to #8, 1XL, turned down eye, Mustad 3906, 3906B
   or 7957B.
Tail: Golden pheasant or two goose biots.
Body: dubbed muskrat fur.
Rib: fine gold tinsel.
Wing: white marabou.
Hackle: Grizzly and brown.

Figure 5-4
Hornberg

Figure 5-5
Marabou Adams

E. Black Midge

This is the fly to use when you can see the fish either breaking or rolling on or at the surface of the water, and everything else you have tried has not triggered a strike. There have been times when the surface of the water looked like rain was falling by the number of rings made by the fish. Yet, the fish would not touch or even nudge any other fly.

This tiny black fluff apparently represents all those little tiny black or gray bugs that are living under the surface and are hardly noticeable to humans. The fish seem to be able to see them. The fish can see them best when they are outlined against the sky. Therefore, you would fish this Black Midge extremely slowly and just below the water's surface. Try to keep the midge one to two inches below the surface of the water.

To keep the midge near the surface empty some of the water out of the bubble. The bubble should almost float. Keep enough water in the bubble so that it will stay just below the surface. The bubble should be trolled so slowly that the bubble does not make a ripple when retrieved.

Black Midge
Hook #12 or #14, 1XS turned down eye, Mustad 7957B, 94848 or 3906.
Tail: None
Body: Black ostrich herl.
Hackle: Short black.

Figure 5-6
Black Midge

F. Black Ant.

The Black Ant represents all of the larger black or gray insects living below the surface. When tied with a soft hackle either at the front or in the middle of the segmented body, it will often produce a striking response in the fish. Because of the Black Ant's distinctive silhouette, at the proper time the Black Ant will be an excellent producer. This fly should be fished slowly with an erratic retrieve.

Black Ant
> Hook: #12 or #14, 2XL, turned down eye, Mustad 9671, 79580, 3906 or 7957B.
> Tail: None.
> Body: Black floss (segmented and lacquered).
> Hackle: Short black at body segment or front.

Figures 5-7
Black Ants

G. Nymph.

The basic nymph pattern represents either the stone fly nymph west of the Mississippi, or perhaps the Hellgrammite east of the Mississippi. The nymph is one of those patterns that the fish sometimes fine irresistible during the period that the nymphs are crawling out from under the rocks, climbing up the seaweed, and getting ready to emerge to the surface and fly away.

Cream, olive, brown, green and gray colors all seem to produce strikes. An examination of the aquatic life of the area you are fishing will probably indicate that most nymphs are colored green or olive. Green and olive colors are usually the most productive. In the very high altitude lakes, above 8,000 feet or above timberline, there are fly hatches of tan or almost white stone flies that resemble a small Miller Moth. In those lakes a small cream or tan nymph is the better producer.

These nymphs are usually fished slowly in spurts that resemble the flight of a nymph from one piece of seaweed to another stalk of seaweed that is six to twelve inches away. Although these nymphs do wiggle mightily, their swimming ability is quite poor and their actual lateral movement is very slow and irregular.

Nymph
> Hook: #10 or #12, 2XL or 3XL, turned down eye, Mustad 9671, 9672 or 79580.
> Tail: 2 or 3 goose biots, green or yellow.
> Body: Green, olive, brown, tan or yellow furry foam strips.
> Rib: Copper wire.
> Hackle: Brown or to match body.
> Thorax: Dark brown tied over hackle.

Figure 5-8
Nymph

H. Black Marabou Streamer

Many of my fly-and-bubble fishing friends swear by the black marabou streamer as the best of all flies for fly-and-bubble fishing. I have also had very good success with it at times. Some writers claim that the Black Marabou Streamer represents a swimming leech. Anyone who has ever seen a leech swimming with its snake-like movement would have a difficult time equating that to the movement of a Marabou Streamer. The secret of tying a good Marabou Streamer is to use at least twice as much marabou as you think you should be using, and then adding on another large clump. If you do not do so, the fly will look like a thin black thread moving through the water. This streamer is best fished in short, quick, stop and go movements.

Black Marabou Streamer
> Hook: #6 or #8, 3XL or 4XL, turned down eye, Mustad, 9672, 3282, 3665A or 79580.
> Tail: None.
> Body: Silver tensil one wrap.
> Wing: Black marabou, very full with six or eight strands of black or green flash.

Figure 5-9
Black Marabou Streamer

I. Marabou Wing Royal Coachman:

The Royal Coachman is one of those flies that I believe was originally tied to catch fishermen, not fish. Nonetheless, it is used all over the world and continues to catch fish when all other patterns fail. This is one fly that you should carry in a large array of sizes. When a size 14 Royal Coachman will not catch a fish, quite often a size 8 will. Some very famous fly fishermen such as Lee Allen, fly tier and author, used the Royal Coachman fly almost exclusively with phenomenal success. For still water fishing, a thick short fluff of white marabou has been substituted for the wings. This fly has traditionally been tied with a few strands of golden pheasant for the tail. Changing the tail by using two or three goose biots would be an interesting variation. The Coachman is fished in slow stop-and-go movements of about six to twelve inches.

Maribou Wing Royal Coachman

    Hook: #8 to #14, 1XL, turned down eye. Mustad 94840 or 7957B.

    Tail: Golden pheasant or two goose biots.

    Body: Segmented, peacock herl front and back and red floss in center.

    Wing: White marabou (short).

    Hackle: Brown saddle.

Figure 5-10
Marabou Wing Royal Coachman

(See page 163 for ordering specially tied flies designed for fly-and-bubble fishing.)

Chapter 6

Be a Detective

A. Study the Aquatic Life

Whether you are going to fish a particular lake or pond regularly, or you are fishing a new lake or pond and would like to have some success immediately, it pays to spend thirty minutes to an hour doing some detective work. The detective work is aimed at finding out what natural sources of fish food are in the lake at that time and what aquatic life is active. This can be done by simply moving slowly and examining the water surface, the items under the water surface, and insects laying on the water.

The most productive examination without equipment is done by simply looking for some floating logs or wood near the shore. Approach the piece of wood with as little disturbance to the water as possible, and very, very slowly turn the log over. The first piece of wood may not produce the information that you are seeking. Once you find a piece of log, stump or wood that have been in the water for a long time, you will find that it usually has nymphs, larvae, leeches, and all forms of aquatic life holding on to its underside.

Anything you find that is large enough to put on a hook can be picked up and used as bait. Examine the log closely and do not shake it or turn it back over too quickly. It may take a minute or two for your eyes to adjust to the insect life on the log, or for an insect to move so that you can see it. It is amazing how nature has camouflaged these insects for survival. When your examination of the log is complete, slowly return the log to its original position. You may be surprised to find that as you turned over the piece of wood, nymphs and other insects crawled around and changed their position as you rolled it over. Every piece of wood contains very small food chain insects that you probably cannot see with the naked eye. These minute life forms live on that log and may be destroyed or killed by sunlight. To protect the delicate balance of the food chain, return the log to its original position.

In the event there are no pieces of submerged wood along the shore, or even if there are and you cannot find the insect life on the wood, you should then examine any of the larger submerged stones along the shore. Again, move through the water slowly and very, very slowly turn over the rock or stone. You should do this so slowly that you do not raise any silt or sand and cloud the water. But even if you do cloud the water, if you stand very still while it clears you may be able to see a variety of insect life on the stone or on the ground where the rock rested under the water.

Any aquatic life big enough to put on a hook can be caught and used as bait. Observing what is under the rocks will give you a clue as to the type of fly to use. Always return the rock to its original position so as not to kill the life both living on the rock and in the soil under the rock. There are often many organisms living there that are sensitive to light. They will quickly die and you can unnecessarily disturb the food chain in the lake if the rock is not returned to its original position.

Another method of examining a body of water and finding its food sources is to locate a seaweed bed close to the shore. Place your arm into the seaweed bed and very slowly pull a portion of the seaweed up onto the shore. Here you must be patient and wait for the water to drain off the seaweed. Until the insect life moves, the small aquatic life is very difficult to see. You will find that the seaweed is literally alive with small insects and crustaceans. In addition, you will also see larger nymphs, leeches, and other underwater life. Slowly go through the seaweed and when your examination is complete, gently return the seaweed to the water to preserve the food chain. After returning the seaweed to the water, carefully examine the ground where the seaweed rested. You should find many organisms that will give you clues as to the type of fly to use. To preserve the food chain, it is imperative that you splash sufficient water where the seaweed had been on the shore. This is to wash these very small item of aquatic life back into the water.

The easiest way to discover the food chain elements in the lake is to construct yourself a sampling net. This is done by taking a long handled landing net and replacing the big mesh with a small mesh minnow net. The small mesh minnow net can be purchased through many of the mail order fishing catalogs. Using this long handled minnow net, it is easy to slowly push the net into the seaweed bed and drag it along the bottom. This procedure will capture much of the food chain life forms in one sweep. When they are in the net, the bugs are easy to examine and remove to use as bait, if large enough. Again, always be certain to reverse the net and swish it back and forth in the water to return the food chain to the water after examination.

Try to match the insect with a fly with the variations stated as the first three "S's" described described in Chapter 4. For those of you who begin to get interested in what is under the surface of the water and how the insects behave, you can make an underwater scope by using a one gallon size plastic bleach bottle. Cut out the bottom as shown in Figure 6-1. Paint the inside of the bottle black. The black paint will keep out the side light. Cover the cut out bottom with heavy plastic wrap and hold the plastic in place with heavy rubber bands. Wade into the water and place the bottom of the scope just below the surface. Move your eye to the top opening so that all light enters from below the surface, see Figure 6-2. When all of the light comes from below the surface, you can clearly see under the surface of the water.

Cut on curve  Heavy rubber band
Heavy plastic wrap

Figure 6-1
Underwater Scope

Figure 6-2
Using the Underwater Scope

Standing in any shallow weed bed peering under the surface, you will be amazed at the insect life and movements that go on. It becomes very fascinating and illustrates the proper fly movements when fishing the fly-and-bubble. People will think you are quite weird when they see you bending over in the water peering into a plastic bleach bottle, but it will all be worthwhile when a little later they see you catching fish while they sit there drowning worms or soaking plastic bait wondering what is wrong and why there are no fish in the lake.

B. Examining the First Fish

The first fish caught will usually make known exactly what the fish are eating if you know the language. The method is simple. Slice the fish from the ventral fin toward the gill. Strip the entrails free, cutting away the pectorals and gill system. Carefully incise the membrane of the stomach, squeeze the contents into your hand for examination. Or in plain language, take a sharp knife, slit open the belly and cut open the heavy intestine that goes from the throat to the digestive tract. Squeeze out the contents into your hand. Don't be squeamish, everything in there is clean. It has been in the water for years. Closely examine the contents. Some items are easy to identify such as crawdads or minnows. If the fish has been feeding on nymphs in the seaweed, the contents can look like green mush. In picking the nymphs off the seaweed the fish will also suck some of the vegetation into its mouth. The fish is not eating the seaweed, it is just taking it in together with the insect it is after. Close examination will permit you to distinguish the seaweed from the insects. Look for color, shape and size. Sometimes only one feature can be the clue which will provide great fishing.

I remember fishing without feeling a bump for over an hour. One of the men in the party finally turned over a rock along the shore, caught a worm, and tried drifting it with a bubble. In a little while he did catch a small fish. We immediately opened it up and examined its internal contents. The fish was full of small orange beetles. We had no idea what they were, but I found an orange and black ant among my flies. That did the trick and I had a couple of hours of great fishing. There are now several small orange flies in my fly box. Too bad I have never caught another fish on an orange fly.

Chapter 7

Reading A Lake

Hundreds of articles and many books have been written concerning reading a stream and anticipating where the fish will be in the stream. You need to know where the fish will most likely be located so that you can make your presentation to the fish and not to empty water. Because the fish are usually not visible, you must be able to anticipate what is below the surface to help decide where to fish. Reading a stream is truly an art, and the experts have refined it to a high degree. Reading a lake is somewhat different than reading a stream and I have never seen a good explanation of how you read a lake. This chapter will provide sufficient basic information to allow you to approach a lake and be able to anticipate what lays below that blanket of water. Once it is understood what is down there below that impenetrable surface, you can make an educated guess as to where and how deep to fish. Figure 7-1, Lake as Normally Observed is located on the next page This shows the typical features seen as you study the shoreline of a lake or reservoir with its mirror surface that hides what is below.

With a little knowledge of geology, hydrology, nature, common sense, and information provided to you in this chapter, you will know a great deal about what to most people is hidden below the glassy surface of the lake. Just by understanding how the area evolved over millions of years, and what happened to the lake after it was filled with water, you will be able to perceive where the fish are most likely suspended and just waiting for an easy meal to come by.

When I look at a lake as shown in Figure 7-1, Lake as Normally Observed and study the clues, I see what is in Figure 7-2, Lake as You Should See It on the following two-page layout.

Picture what is in Figure 7-2, and will know where to find the fish and why you should fish there.

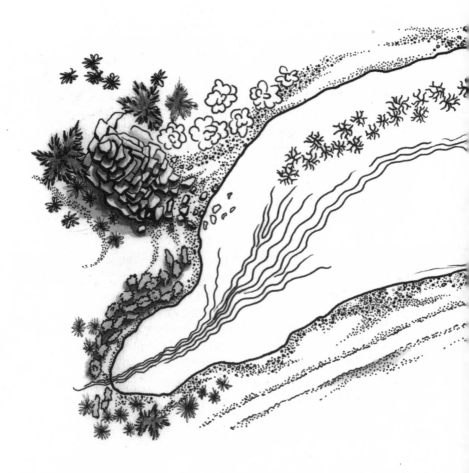

Point D

Figure 7-1
Lake as Normally Observed

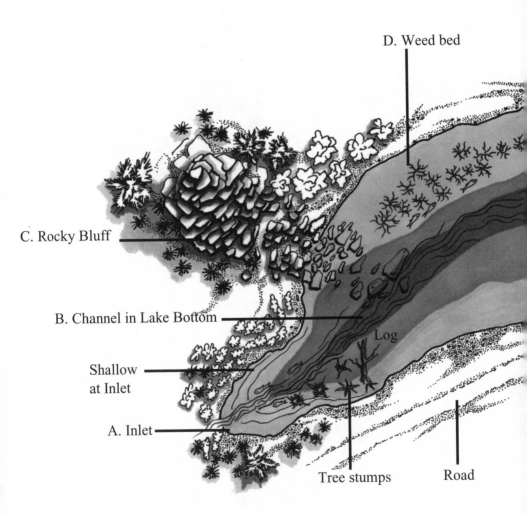

D. Weed bed

C. Rocky Bluff

B. Channel in Lake Bottom

Log

Shallow
at Inlet

A. Inlet

Tree stumps

Road

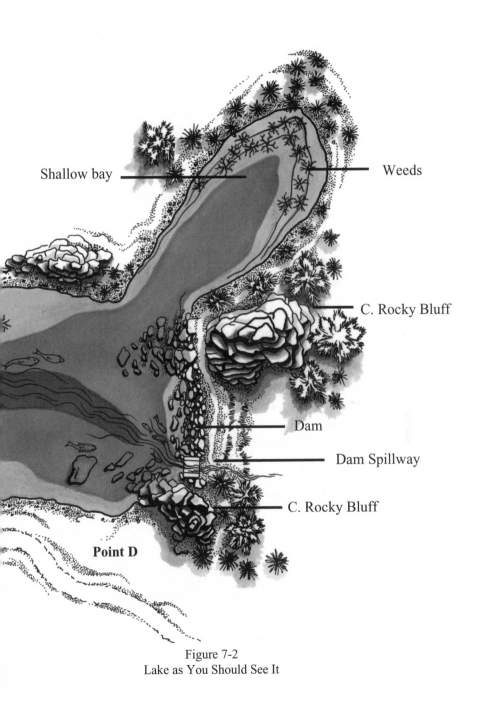

Shallow bay

Weeds

C. Rocky Bluff

Dam

Dam Spillway

C. Rocky Bluff

Point D

Figure 7-2
Lake as You Should See It

A. Inlets

Most lakes have an inlet. If they do not have an inlet, they probably have an underground spring located somewhere in the lake that brings in fresh water. There are many lakes and reservoirs that contain both inlets and springs.

The power of flowing water is incredible. Very large rocks can be moved by an unbelievably small flow of water. The rock is lighter under water by the amount of water it displaces. A cubic foot of rock weighs the weight of the rock out of the water, less the weight of each cubic foot of water it displaces. A very large rock can be moved or rolled down hill by a small amount of water. The same physical laws hold true for everything in the water or on the water. This permits the water to move objects on the surface or beneath the surface.

As the flowing water reaches the still water of the lake, it meets resistance to its flow as it now has to push the still water. In addition, as the flowing water is no longer retained by the banks of the stream it spreads out. As the water spreads it loses velocity. The loss of velocity causes the substances in the water to sink to the bottom and stop moving. Not only rocks and heavy items, but water-soaked logs, sand, soil, silt, and anything that is not floating on the surface sink to the bottom as the speed of the water slows down.

This deposit of debris causes the inlet portion of the lake to become shallow as it fills with dirt and silt. The inlet also fills with objects such as logs, rocks and debris which provide protection and food for the fish. The sunken objects provide protection and the flow provides food on which the fish can feed. That is why there are often fish rising at the inlet of a lake when they are not rising in any other part of the lake.

Many species of fish must spawn in the moving water. The moving water is highly aerated and provides needed oxygen for the fish eggs to hatch. During the spawning season adult fish tend to congregate near the inlet to lay their eggs in the current. The inlet has the only moving water in a lake or reservoir. If you hit it right, all of large fish in the lake may be lying at the inlet trying to spawn.

If the water is too shallow, the fish will not move to the inlet until it is covered by shadow as the fish have a genetically programmed protective device to keep it out of shallow water when the light is bright. While the surface of the water is still bathed in sunlight the fish is prone to attack from above by eagle or osprey. Again, this hesitancy of the fish to get near the surface in sunlight is not a mental thought of the fish, or fear, but rather the fish has evolved with this protective mechanism in its genes.

This evolution took thousands of years using the process called natural selection. Those fish that came near the surface during bright sunlight were simply caught and eaten by eagle and osprey. A fish cannot propagate inside a birds stomach, therefore those fish did not reproduce to pass on the genes that insured survival. Those fish that stayed out of shallow water or near the surface of the water during bright sunny days reproduced. Over the centuries only those fish that had the genetic trait of staying out of shallow water in bright light survived to reproduce and pass on the trait.

B. Channels in the Lake Bottom

Whether the lake is man-made or natural, there is probably a definite old river channel in the bottom of the lake. Man-made lakes are usually built in canyons or ravines which have been created and cut by thousands of years of flowing water. The river channel will normally be the deepest portion of the lake and also provide some form of drop-off next to which the fish tend to hide and congregate.

Common sense will tell you that the channel has to be located between the inlet and the outlet. In the event there are two outlets, there will be two channels with the deeper one or primary one indicated by the deeper ravine behind the outlet. That is where most of the water has flowed over the centuries and therefore the flowing water has cut a deeper channel and ravine.

When surveying a man-made lake which has two dams, the taller dam would indicate the location of the outlet of the main channel and the shorter dam would indicate the location of the secondary channel. To determine which dam is taller you need only to examine the side of the dam that is not covered with water. The secondary channel would have been created when the water for any reason was permitted to rise high enough to cut a second outlet. Clues as to where these channels are located in the body of the lake are described in the next few sections.

C. Rocky Bluffs or Points

Most fisherman automatically step onto the rocky bluff or point and cast out from it. They do this even though they cannot see what is below the surface of the water. A study of rocky bluffs and points that are not covered with water will quickly show what is below the water surface. Just because you cannot see what's down there doesn't mean you cannot know what is down there.

The rocky bluffs and points were created by many thousands of years of geological activity. Rocks that eventually have their underpinnings eroded roll down the bluff into the valley. When the water fills up the valley, the rocks are still there. The process does not stop just because the canyon has been filled with water, but continues on forever. Even when the lake is full rocks become loose and continue to roll down the steep bluffs and into the water.

The rocks below the water surface provide a great deal of cover, food and protection for the fish. Fish the rocky points moving your lure between the rocks or bouncing the lure on and off the rocks. The fish are just laying there waiting for something to come by as genetic programming has ingrained this pattern within them. A steep rocky drop-off at the waters shoreline probably means that the stream has cut away the bluff. That is likely the location of one point of the stream bed.

D. Weed beds

Weed beds within the lake provide data as to the contour of the bottom of the lake. The many varieties of seaweed have different requirements as to light and soil. The available light required for seaweed growth diminishes as the water gets deeper. That is why there are different types of seaweed or water growth at different depths in the lake.

A definite seaweed line means that there is a sudden change of depth in the bottom of the lake. The visible weeds probably cannot grow in the deeper water. As illustrated in Figure 7-2, the sudden change of depth was caused by the old river bed. Fishing along a seaweed bed is usually productive, but can be especially rewarding for catching large fish. The drop-off not only provides the fish a ready food supply from the seaweed bed, but also the protection of the deeper water.

Fish tend to lie along the edge of seaweed bed waiting to ambush a nymph, minnow, or any underwater food item. The food may move away from the seaweed bed and be quickly taken by the fish, or the movement within the seaweed can be seen by the fish and the strike mechanism of the fish kicks in and it takes the food. Quite often the food is taken right off of the seaweed which means that some seaweed is also taken into the fish's digestive system. If you have ever cleaned a fish and cut open its belly and seen it full of seaweed, that is what has happened. The fish are not eating seaweed, they are simply taking the food item off the seaweed and ingesting a certain amount of seaweed with the food.

E. Springs

It is usually very difficult to locate fresh water springs within a lake. If it is a man-made lake there may be old USGS (United States Geological Survey) maps available showing the location of springs. People familiar with the area prior to the construction of the lake can also lead to the location of springs.

A hole in the weed bed will often be a clue as to the location of the underground spring. The spring water can exert enough pressure from below to move the soil out and deepen the area where the spring is located. Because of the increased depth and looseness of the soil, underwater growth will not always be able to survive in the area of the spring.

Clearer water in an area can indicate the presence of an underground spring. This would be more visible when the lake is cloudy with silt or other runoff or in a lake that contains algae. The spring water will be noticeably clearer where the pure water is rising out of the bottom and moving the dirty water or algae to the side.

Fishing in a spring hole can be productive for the same reason that fishing next to a weed bed can be rewarding. I have seen times that the fish will be rising in a large spring hole, and rising in no other place in the lake.

F. Side Canyons and Ravines

Some shore lines contain a side canyon or ravine leading into the lake. Just because the water starts at the shore line does not mean that the canyon or ravine does not continue into the lake. These underwater canyons and ravines can be the lair of very large fish. Locate the cut and fish right into its deepest part.

Chapter 8

Proper Fishing Methods

A. Never Twist a Rod

Rods are designed to bend. It makes no difference if a rod is constructed of bamboo, fiberglass, boron, composite, or steel, it is not made to withstand twisting. Twisting is a sure way to rupture the fibers and weaken the rod. You can be certain that the weakened rod will fail as soon as you have a trophy fish on the other end. No matter what the situation, NEVER TWIST A ROD! To help in meeting the dictates of this rule follow the suggestions stated below.

There will be no tendency to twist the rod if it is assembled correctly in the first place and then have some special knowledge of how to take it apart when the rod is stubborn and stuck together.

Lubricate the male ferrule before you push it into the female ferrule. The perfect lubricant is with you at all times. It is the body oil just below your ear on your cheek and neck. Simply rub the male ferrule along that area with a rolling motion and the ferrule will be properly oiled. See Figure 8-1, Lubricating the Ferrule.

For those who like to be handy around the house, use the same trick when replacing a light bulb. Before putting the new bulb in the socket simply roll the threads in the same place on your face and neck. When you have to replace the bulb a year or so later you will find that the small amount of body oil will make the bulb easy to remove.

B. Assembly and Disassembly of the Rod.

Even after lubricating the male ferrule they sometimes get wedged in tighter than you can pull apart. This is when there is the tendency to twist the rod to loosen the joint. DO NOT TWIST! Sufficient tension to pull the rod apart can almost always be generated by placing the rod behind your back and leveraging your arm strength. See Figure 8- 2, Disassembling the Rod.

Figure 8-1
Lubricating the Ferrule

Figure 8-2
Disassembling the Rod

Place the rod behind you, rod handle down. For right handers, place your left hand on the bottom portion with thumb pointed up. Place your right hand on the top portion with thumb pointed up. With your right elbow pointed down you will produce tremendous tensile pressure on the rod and pull it apart.

C. Holding the Rod While Fishing.

This is fly rod fishing and you should hold the rod as you would in normal fly fishing, reel at the butt and dominant hand on the grip. The reel crank should be located on the side where the nondominant hand can do the retrieving. You do not change hands after the cast to retrieve the line or to fight the fish, but use normal fly rod fishing positions. Keep the right hand on the grip and use the left hand to operate the reel. Unlike fly fishing, you retrieve the line and fight the fish by using the crank of the reel. Do not try to land the fish by pulling the line with your hand or fingers. There will be too much line out to use this method and a large fish can pull hard enough to cut your hand with the thin line. See Figure 8-3, Holding the Line.

D. Movement of the Fly

If you have gone through the effort of studying the actions of the life under the surface of the water, you will realize that everything under the surface moves very, very slowly. The smaller the object, the slower it moves through the water. Fish, being the top of the food chain move quickly so as to feed on the slower moving life forms. The smaller insects may wiggle violently, but they do not move fast in any direction. See Figure 8-4, Movement of the Fly.

To trigger the strike mechanism of a fish, your fly should move slowly through the water. Further study of the movement of the underwater life, shows aquatic life does not move very far without stopping. The exception is during a fly hatch where the nymphs are trying to reach the shore or any other dry object. Then, they can crawl out of the water, split their cases, and emerge in the winged form called *emergers*.

Normally an insect will only move from one place of hiding or feeding to another. Movement of these insects is usually six to twelve inches. That is about the length of movement your fly should move without slowing to a virtual stop or fully stopping.

This stop-and-go method adds life-like movement to the fly. To actually see the effect of the water on the fly, take a fly and attach it to a piece of leader. Place the fly in a bathtub, sink or an aquarium. Move the fly through the water in a stop-and-go action. Notice that as you move the fly forward the water pressure causes the feathers and body material to contract around the body. When the fly stops, the feathers expand out again. This movement of the materials give the fly a lifelike, breathing action. It is common to feel the strike as the fly stops and the its feathers expand making the fly look alive.

E. Depth of Fishing

As previously discussed, it is seldom that fish actually take insects off the surface of the water in bodies of still water. That is because there are seldom insects on the surface of the water. Even during the middle of a fly hatch when the insects are on the surface, they have arrived there by coming from below. The fish will feed on the nymphs before they ever reach the surface. For every rise seen on the surface of the water, there are probably a hundred insects taken below that rise. Obviously, you want to fish where the most feeding is taking place.

During the course of a very active fly hatch indicated by many insects on the surface and boils made by rising fish, it is best to fish about six to twelve inches below the surface. Just below the surface is where the fish are working free of the hindrance of weed beds and the insects are in full view of the fish. The best vision of the fish is straight out from the eyes and above. Even in bad light a fish can see an object outlined against the sky. See Figure 8-4, Depth of Fishing.

Fish, like most wild animals, spend most of their life eating or looking for food. Although there are certainly times when the fish will go to the bottom of a lake and not move, this is actually quite rare. Most of the time the fish are eating or looking for food somewhere in the lake. It is up to you to find them and properly present the fly to get a strike.

When the fish are not actively feeding near the surface making swirls that the fish make while feeding, the fish are often lying just

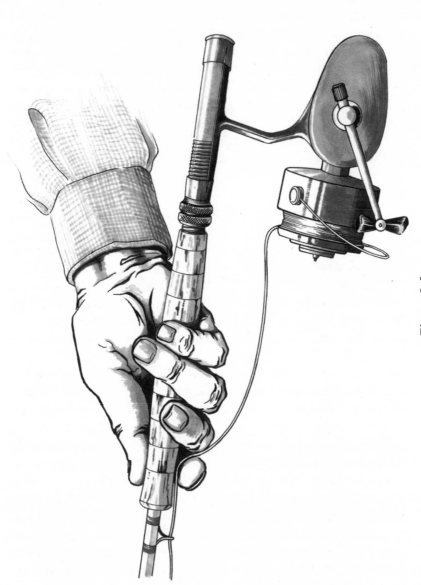

Figure 8-3
Holding the Line

below the top of the weed beds. This allows the fish to stay in one position and still see food items moving from weed to weed.

The fish can also see above them, outlined against the sky, any food item that moves out of the weed bed and into their strike zone. The fly must be in the fish's strike zone, it is very important to adjust the weight of the bubble and the speed of the retrieve to keep the fly just above the weed bed. A properly fished fly-and-bubble will actually touch the top of the weeds where the fish are lying as you retrieve the fly.

F. Adjusting the Depth of the Fly-and-Bubble

The plastic of the bubbles is slightly heavier than water. Therefore the bubble will sink if it is full of water. The problem is that it sinks very slowly. Because of the upward angle of the fishing line during the retrieve the line is always drawing the bubble toward the surface. This upward pull makes it difficult to keep the bubble deep with only water in the bubble.

An easy solution is to put something heavier than water or plastic into the bubble. Six or eight pieces of lead shot will usually do the trick. The amount of lead shot needed will depend upon the size of the shot. With lead shot in the bubble the bubble will sink faster and also make the bubble sink and hold its position every time you slow your retrieve or stop.

Another advantage of using a weighted bubble is that there is no need to weigh the fly. That is, place extra weight on the fly's hook to make it sink. By putting weight in the bubble and not the fly you can bounce the bubble on the bottom of the lake or tip the top of the weeds and still keep the fly just above the bottom of the lake or just above the weeds where the fish can clearly see the fly. This greatly improves your chance of getting a strike.

By properly holding the line so that it slips through your fingers as it is being retrieved, you can often feel the bubble bouncing off the bottom of the lake or touching the top of the weeds. When you get those sensations, you are most likely going to get a strike.

G. Holding the Line

The proper method of holding the line is by running the line across the index finger while retrieving it as shown in Figure 8-3. Holding the line by this method will become automatic with practice.

Catching the line with the index finger can be a problem with open-faced reels where the bail swings the line away from the finger. This rotation will cause the line to hit the back of your hand when the handle is turned. Reels that turn the line toward the open finger make it easy to just reach down with the index finger and catch the line as you turn the handle. After catching the line with your index finger you can then bring it up to proper position.

The finger on your line is your communication system between you, the bubble and the fly. That is how to sense if a fish has struck the fly and if the bubble is touching the weeds. This method also permits you to instantaneously tighten the finger against the grip with the line in between and hold the line tight against the grip. Then you can bring up the rod tip to set the hook firmly into the fish's mouth.

H. Rod Tip Angle and Setting the Hook

Normal fly rod fishing is "loose line fishing." That is, the line is laying loose on the water. In "loose line" fishing it is common to aim the tip of the rod at the fly, or to point the tip of the rod where the line enters the water. This gives the conventional fly fisherman the opportunity to take up additional slack when he sees a strike take place. In regular fly fishing there is no feel of the strike, you can only see it.

Fly-and-bubble fishing is tight line fishing, and pointing the rod tip at the bubble or the fly gives no advantages. Here you want maximum touch and feel of the line which requires an angle between the line and the rod. The amount of the angle is not critical but should be held somewhere between 30 and 90 degrees as shown in Figure 8-5, Rod Tip Angle. This helps you feel the delicate pulls and tugs that are going on between you and the fly-and-bubble.

As the line is already tight it is not necessary to move the rod tip a long distance to set the hook. In tight line fishing, moving the rod tip back a foot or two is usually sufficient to firmly set the hook into the fish. The setting of the hook should not be violent, but a

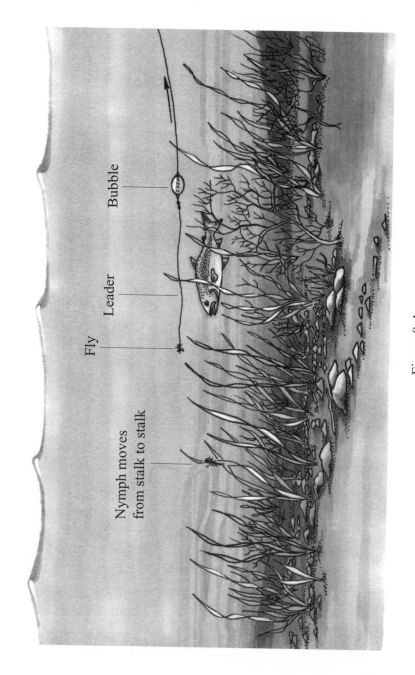

Figure 8-4
Movement of the Fly and Depth of Fishing

smooth, firm motion as shown in Figure 8-5, Rod Tip Angle and Setting the Hook.

It is more comfortable to retrieve the line with your rod held to the side and almost horizontally. If your bubble or fly is constantly being tugged by underwater growth, the problem can often be corrected by simply raising the rod tip to a more vertical position. This technique changes the angle of retrieve and pulls the bubble and fly a little higher each time the bubble is moved toward you. See Figure 8-6, Line Angle.

Using this trick of varying the height of your rod tip above the water can keep your fly-and-bubble just above the weed bed without changing the amount of water in your bubble.

I. Wind

It is common knowledge that fish tend to face upstream. The fish have been programmed to take this position so that they can see food that is drifting to them while remaining stationary. Fish also tend to face the wind. The wind will set up slight currents that are imperceptible to humans, but are very apparent to the fish. The wind also drifts surface food down wind. If the fish are facing into the wind they can see the food drifting toward them.

Cast into the wind in still water fishing. As the wind velocity increases, so does the tendency of the fish to face into it. Because of this natural trait of fish it is better to cast into the wind than with the wind. The cast into the wind will draw the fly toward the front of the fish and into the fish's strike zone. The fish sees the fly sooner and the fly is more likely to trigger a strike. A fly cast with the wind or downwind is more likely to pass over the fish from behind. The fly approaching the fish from behind places the fly in a smaller strike zone and sight zone of the fish. Figure 8-4, Movement of the Fly.

Casting into the wind is more difficult but most of this problem can be alleviated by learning to use the side arm cast. A low side arm cast keeps the fly-and-bubble low to the water and out of the strongest wind.

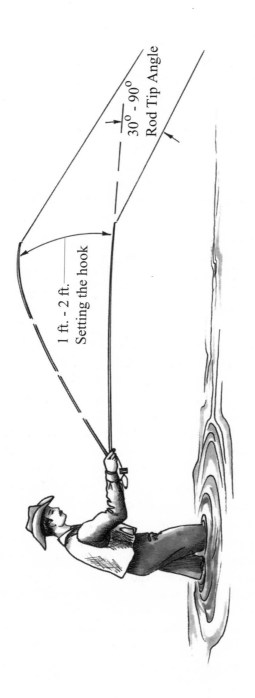

Rod Tip Angle

$30^{\circ} - 90^{\circ}$

1 ft. - 2 ft.
Setting the hook

Figure 8-5
Rod Tip Angle and Setting the Hook

J. Fish under the Birds

Salt water fisherman have always cast to the birds feeding on the surface of the water. Those birds are probably feeding on bait fish being driven up to the surface by larger fish just below them. In fresh water, the birds are sending you a similar signal. Whenever you see birds flying along the surface, dipping to the surface or just swooping around an area of the lake, it is probably because a fly hatch has started or the nymphs are beginning to move below the surface prior to a fly hatch. The birds sense this activity and proceed to that area in order to eat the same insects on which the fish feed. Only those insects that escape the fish reach the surface of the water. Just put your fly below the birds and the fish should be there also.

Just before dark not only the birds will feed right at the surface, but so will the bats and night hawks. The bats are equally sensitive to a fly hatch which has just started or is just about to start. Fishing under those areas of feeding birds and bats is usually productive.

K. Cast to the Rises

The one way you can be certain that there are fish where you are casting is to cast where the fish are rising or in some way disturbing the water surface and signaling their presence. At those times, it is best to cast just beyond the water disturbance and bring your fly slowly over the area where the swirl took place. Studies of fish feeding patterns show the fish will rise to the surface or just at the surface, take the food, and then turn and slowly swim away. If your cast is slightly off to one side, you still have a fifty percent chance of putting your fly in the strike zone of that fish.

When fish are disturbing the water surface, do not assume they are feeding on insects floating on the surface. Watch the surface intensely to try to discover what is creating the disturbance. It may be a tail or a dorsal fin which would mean the fish are actually taking food six inches to a foot below the surface.

Anything on the surface or flying just above the surface will give you clues as to the hatch. As Ernest Schwiebert's famous book states: *Match the Hatch.* In the event your cast lands between three or four rises and still you do not get a strike within three or four casts, it is time to change your fly to a different variation of either size,

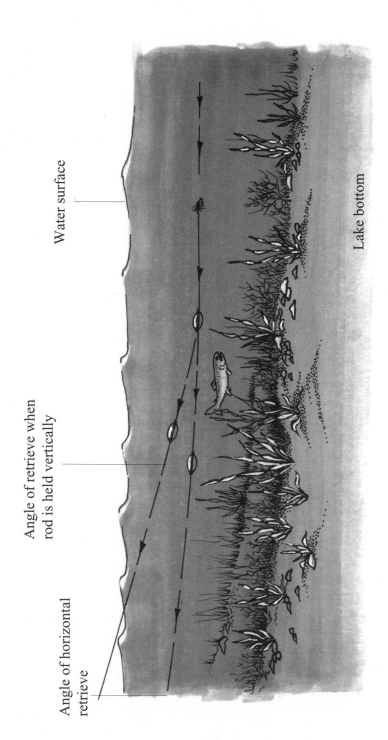

Water surface

Lake bottom

Angle of retrieve when
rod is held vertically

Angle of horizontal
retrieve

Figure 8-6
Line Angle

shade, or silhouette as discussed in Chapter 5. When the fish are actively feeding and rising you should have a strike at least every other cast.

In the event you have tried all of the variations of flies and do not get a strike, change the speed of your retrieve or change the method of retrieve to steady, fast and slow, fast and stop, or some other variation that may trigger the striking instinct of the fish. If you are not catching with the method you are using—CHANGE!

L. Casting Patterns

The smart fisherman, when fishing blind, who is not having any particular reason to believe that there are fish in the precise area where he is fishing, uses a casting pattern that effectively covers all of the water around him. As shown in Figure 8-7, Casting Patterns, a fisherman standing on the shore at position one (P1) would start fishing by casting to the right and making five to six casts across the area. Each cast going in a counter-clockwise direction to cover the whole area reachable from that position. This covers the water in a fanning arc.

A school of fish may be located at position A and moving to the left. The fisherman would then move to position 2 (P2) and start the same pattern. As shown by the diagram, the school of fish that originally were in position A are now in position B, and the first cast from position 2 (P2) will be in the fish's strike zone. In addition, any other fish lying in the area will have the fly go over them from one position or the other and you are more likely to put your presentation within the fish's strike zone. This method permits coverage of all the water in front of you and makes it more likely that you will put your fly before a fish.

If you catch a fish or get a strike while fishing blind, immediately cast again to the same location. You may have found a school of feeding fish and should keep working them. Studies have shown that thirty percent of the school of fish can caught before the fish stop striking.

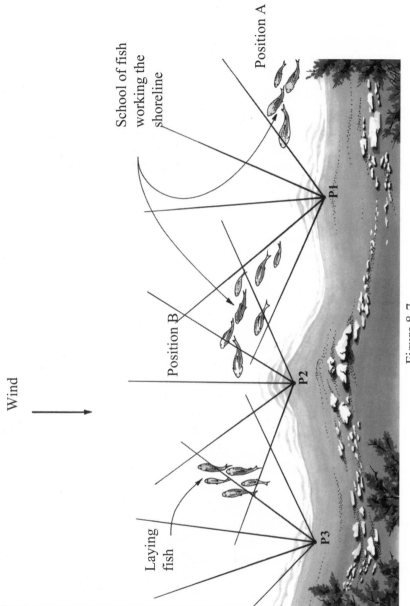

Wind

School of fish working the shoreline

Position A

Position B

Laying fish

P1

P2

P3

Figure 8-7
Casting Patterns

M. Fish Every Cast

All fishermen make casts that land way off of the intended target. No matter where in the water the cast lands, fish it as though it were the perfect cast. You do not know where a fish is lying, you can only guess.

All animals are little balls of pure positive energy. Send out good vibrations when fishing. There is no method of determining if good feelings will get more fish, but my observations make me believe that those fishermen who hold good expectations and positive thoughts do catch more fish and have a better time while fishing.

One of my favorite episodes involved my son, Greg, and his then girlfriend, Jeannie. They had been high school sweethearts and were both attending the same college. Things were getting serious. They both love skiing and had that in common, but downhill skiing is a winter sport and the other six or seven months of the year Greg loved to fish. Jeannie came from an old fashion Greek family that believed girls should stay home and raise lots of babies. Although Jeannie had several brothers she never had the opportunity to do such "man things" as fishing.

"Dad, I want to take Jeannie fishing. Where can we go and be sure Jeannie catches a lot of fish and has a good time?"

"Let me see what I can come up with," I answered. A friend of mine had just purchased a building lot in a high mountain subdivision. The subdivision contained a small private lake of about six acres. The lot ownership gave him the right to join the fishing association and fish the lake. He said the lake was well stocked and was located in a beautiful scenic area. He delivered to me three guest passes and a key to the gate. The plan was to arrive after lunch, give Jeannie a chance to learn to cast while standing on the shore and then spend the evening fishing.

Within one hour Jeannie was making consistent casts with the fly-and-bubble. My son or I would stand next to her and give gentle instructions. The other would fish a few feet away and when hooking into a fish would hand the rod over to Jeannie to give her the thrill of the fight. Jeannie was thoroughly enjoying all the attention and the excitement of landing the fish.

The evening sun was near the top of the pine trees lining the south and west sides of the lake. A few fish were beginning to rise along the edge of the weed bed lying along the south shore. Everything was going according to plan. We turned the rowboat upright and the oars were under the boat as we had been told. The boat was left to drift about fifty feet from the edge of the weed bed where the fish were now actively rising. A thick mat of weeds lay on the surface of the water starting at the south shore and extending out about thirty feet. Greg and I feathered our cast with our left hand, stopping the bubble about eight feet from the weed bed. The slowing of the bubble permitted the fly to shoot forward and land at the edge of the weeds.

The fish were active. Greg and I were getting strikes every cast. If we missed the first bump, another fish would strike within a few feet. The fish were running twelve to sixteen inches in length and roughly one to two pounds each.

Jeannie was not having much luck. Her casting was not yet so sophisticated as to be able to control the length of her cast. Her line frequently got hung up in the weeds and without complaining, she tried to drag her fly or bubble through the weeds and get it loose. Suddenly, she turned her body to face the open water and let loose with a long cast. I looked over at Jeannie and in my most polite, calm and fatherly voice said, "Jeannie when the fish are working . . ." Her rod doubled over as she was into a real fish. After many "Hold up your rod tip" and other advice which I am sure she did not hear anyway, Greg slipped the net under a beautiful, fat three and one-half pound rainbow trout.

We had been releasing all the fish unharmed as is the polite thing to do when fishing someone else's private lake. This fish we had to keep. Greg also kept two eight or nine inch fish. The photograph of this trip shows Greg with a pout on his face holding up his two eight or nine inch fish and Jeannie beaming her beautiful smile, holding up that three and one-half pound trout. Jeannie and Greg are now married and living with my beautiful granddaughter, Demetra, in Aspen, Colorado where they ski all winter and fish the rest of the year.

N. New Lake Fishing Procedure

Let's take you through a typical fishing scenario where you pull up to a new lake as shown on Figure 7-1, Lake as Normally Observed. You pull off the road, park at point D, step out of your vehicle, remove your rod and start fishing with the same fly you were using the last place you fished.

You survey the lake and now see what is on Figure 7-2, Lake as You Should See It. The first cast in your casting pattern is to the right and is going to be over rocks off the rocky point. The depth of the water is unknown but by the slant of the shore you guess the water is five feet deep at the spot your bubble lands. You let the full bubble sink for four seconds (a count of four). A slow, stop and go retrieve and nothing, no fish, no strikes, no weeds, nothing.

The next cast in your casting pattern, Figure 8-7, you let the bubble sink seven seconds and bump into a rock. The third cast you let sink eight seconds and you get a strike. Two more casts in the same area where you got the bump are without further results and you continue in your casting pattern. You now know what to expect and let each cast on you casting pattern sink a little deeper until you have reached straight out from your position. At that point your future casts will be landing in shallower water as you proceed to cast back towards the shore. Now the sinking time of the bubble on each cast is decreased. Of course, once you have a strike, additional casts are made in the same area at that depth or deeper in the hope that you are into a school of feeding fish.

Chapter 9

The Secret - Visualization

When my son was eight years old he could stand near three or four other fly-and-bubble fisherman and consistently catch fish when they only had an occasional strike. Often when I would do that, people would come over to me and ask what I was using, what I was doing or otherwise try to find out why I was catching fish and they weren't? Many times I would attempt to explain to them what I was doing, but usually I did not have much success in adequately describing my method in such a manner as to improve their success.

The publisher of this book kept giving me those, "yeah, I believe your fish story" looks as I would describe my fishing success to him. He began to take serious notice of my fishing stories as I offered, and then brought him substantial quantities of large trout for his dinner on a regular basis. But he was still a little skeptical of my method realizing that some people are just plain lucky. Finally, I offered to take him fishing with me.

We went to one of my favorite locations and I set him up with the same rod, reel, bubble, leader and fly as I was using. I described to him my fishing method and we stood approximately forty feet apart casting into the same water.

Every second or third cast, I had a fish on my line. Jack occasionally had a strike and landed two or three fish during the three to four hours we fished. During this fishing session I had the feeling that either I had not rigged him up properly, or I was just simply fishing in the right spot. We exchanged gear and location. Immediately I was getting a fish every second or third cast standing in his spot using the rod, reel and fly he had just been using. Jack had moved to my spot, and using my outfit, was only getting an occasional strike. We exchanged again with the same results.

He was getting frustrated and was willing to acknowledge that I was the better fisherman. I was equally frustrated as I knew that my method should work for everyone and that he should be catching just as many fish as I was catching.

For a week after that trip, I pondered as to why I was catching fish and Jack wasn't. I knew that my son could stand next to me and do just as well as I did, and yet I could not figure out any way to describe what I was doing in such terms so that someone else could understand it. For a week I mulled over this dilemma and finally came up with the solution. *Visualization.* I excitedly called Jack on the phone and said, "Come on, let's go try the same place again and see if we can find a way to have you catch your share of the fish." Jack was more than willing to take another fishing trip and we set it up for the following week.

We went to the same spot on the same lake with the same equipment and I said to Jack, "After you let that fly drop to the top of the weed bed, as you reel in the line, picture that fly in your mind, swimming slowly from one stalk of seaweed to the next stalk which is about six to twelve inches away. Actually see that small insect in your mind letting loose of one piece of seaweed, turning, swimming along, grabbing onto another stalk of seaweed and holding on, then picture that insect leaving that piece of seaweed swimming along, grabbing another piece of seaweed and holding on. Move that fly using the handle of your reel. Do that all the way into shore and see what happens." That afternoon, I roughly counted: Jack caught 24 trout and I caught 20.

Visualization techniques are a method used by all pro athletes and most of the good college athletes, dancers and any individual who wants to perform to their maximum potential. It permits your mind to direct your body to act in a manner that gives you peak performance. It is the same in fishing. Visualizing the movement of the fly through the water, and even visualizing the trout swimming up to the fly, putting its nose right up to the fly, opening its mouth, and then opening its gills to suck in the fly helps in catching fish. Using this technique in all fishing, whether it be flies, lures, or even bait, will greatly improve your catches.

No one actually knows how visualization techniques work. Many theorizes exists. Some believe that you are reaching you inner self, your higher being, the universal mind, that it is actually a prayer being answered by God or just your subconscious doing what is necessary to be successful. It really doesn't make any difference what makes the process work. The only important factors are that it does work for most people and that it cannot do you any harm. Some people I know would say you are just sending out good "vibes" and that is why this method is successful. I don't know if that is true, but it certainly does not hurt to fish with a happy, positive attitude.

Of equal importance with the visualization method is the fact that to catch fish you simply must go fishing. To enjoy fishing you must do it. Don't be concerned by time of year, time of day, weather conditions or any other factor, just simply go fishing and have a good time. It is a positive, absolute, scientific fact and law of the universe that every hour you spend fishing adds an hour to your life. Therefore when you go fishing you do not take time away from your family, your work, or anyone else. You just gain another hour to spend with your family, or your job at some later point of your life. No one loses anything and everyone gains a more pleasant, happy, relaxed individual to be around.

Chapter 10

Dress and Safety

Your first impression of someone you meet is probably largely based upon the way they are dressed. People who are improperly dressed for the activity in which they are engaged, make it clear that they do not have the experience to understand what they are doing and get little respect.

Every activity has appropriate dress, whether it be for convenience, by tradition or for safety reasons. When it comes to fishing, the appropriate dress is dictated by both health and safety. Go up to the shoreline and see someone running around in the undergrowth wearing sneakers without socks, shorts and a tank top. You know immediately that he is a real tenderfoot. They are also a safety threat to themselves and to everyone else.

The first time that "tenderfoot" steps out of the water with a large black leech attached firmly to his ankle, he will understand why he should not go wading in the water without some protection. Additionally when that person gets home covered with chigger bites, ticks with their heads buried into his skin, welts from mosquitoes and toasted from too much sun, he will understand why people dress properly when communing with nature.

The properly attired fisherman is well protected from the soles of his feet to the top of his head from all of the little nasties that nature can throw at him. Experienced outdoorsmen and fisherman are dressed in similar fashion. Not all experienced fishermen dress the same but you can certainly spot one as soon as you see him. Their basic rules are as follows:

A. Footwear

Hip boots or chest waders are always preferred when you are going to enter the water or walk through heavy undergrowth. They keep you dry, comfortable and protected from not only such underwater threats as leeches, but also snake bites or other dangers. In the event that waders or hip boots are not practical, at least wear high socks under your shoes and tightly attach the bottom of your heavy trousers to your legs and ankles with string or large rubber bands. This will limit access to your skin by all the little creatures that nature has put out there to feed on soft-skinned humans.

B. Pants
Your pants should be of neutral color and of heavy twill or duck material. The material should be tough enough to withstand and keep out such nuisances as mosquitoes.

C. Shirts
Wear at least two layers of covering above the waist. The outer shirt should be of neutral color and made of a material thick enough to withstand and keep out such biting insects as mosquitoes. A cotton undershirt or T-shirt will help you keep warm in cold weather. By absorbing perspiration and then evaporating the moisture, it will also keep you cooler in hot weather.

D. Eye Wear
Never, never go fishing without wearing something to protect your eyes! If you ever have the misfortune of seeing someone with a fishhook stuck in their eyeball you will certainly never forget it. Do not risk that happening to you.

I had that unfortunate experience once when taking one of my small children to the emergency room of a hospital. In the emergency room was a young man with a treble hook attached to a small bass plug with one barb of the treble hook firmly imbedded in the young man's eyeball. I did check at a later date and discovered he suffered no permanent eye damage. The mere sight of that hook and plug sticking out of his eye made me realize that could have been me, my son or some innocent bystander. This was an immediate learning experience. It's an experience that lasts a lifetime.

During daylight hours, polarized eye wear can bring much enjoyment to fishing. The polarization permits you to see past the surface glare and into the water. During twilight or darkness if you do not wear clear glasses, you should wear some form of safety glasses when fishing. Accidents can and do happen, even to you. Do not take any risk that can seriously injure your eyes.

E. Headgear

Your headgear should be a wide brimmed hat. Although it is fashionable at the present time to wear baseball caps, they are not practical headgear for fishing or any other outdoor activity other than baseball. The wide brimmed hat protects your face, ears, neck, and other exposed upper body parts from the sun. In addition during rains, the wide brimmed hat deflects the rain off of your face and neck onto your shoulders or back. Most importantly the wide brimmed hat protects your neck, ears, eyes and head from the barbed hooks flying around your body when fishing.

An added feature to the wide brimmed hat is that it can repel flying and biting insects using insect repellent, without putting the repellent directly on your skin. You can effectively repel insects by simply spraying or squirting the repellent on the underside of the brim of the hat. Be careful not to get the repellent on the flies, as there is reason to believe that the insect repellent not only repels insects, but also repels fish.

F. Tools

Never go fishing without a pair of long-nosed pliers or forceps on your person.

Leaving work at noon to spend an afternoon fishing a small quiet lake during the middle of the week was a wonderful idea. I pushed the rowboat off the shore and just as I hoped, there was not another person anywhere near the lake. It was the middle of the afternoon, the sun was shining, the birds were singing, the water was calm, there were no fish working. The pleasant squeaking of the oars as I rowed around trolling a small wobbling lure holding two treble hooks on a spreader was a peaceful way to spend the afternoon.

The rod was held in a rod holder as I slowly trolled the lure along the edge of a weed bed that had reached to the water's surface.

Suddenly the rod tip was in the water and shaking violently. I grabbed the pole and set the hook. It was a stout fish that made several nice long runs and certainly earned its freedom. I don't usually keep but one fish for dinner, so I had planned to release this large fish. A three pound rainbow trout is too much for me to eat. The fish fought itself into exhaustion and was lying on its side. I pulled the fish along the surface to the side of the boat to unhook it. One of the treble hooks was imbedded deep in its throat. The forceps are always kept hooked to a high pocket flap on the left side of my fishing vest. I reached for the forceps planning to remove the hook from the fish without touching the fish or even taking the fish out of the water. The forceps were not there.

Now, removing the hook from the fish while the fish was in the boat seemed easier, so the fish was netted and laid at my feet in the boat. Looking into the mouth I could see that two of the hooks of the treble hooks were deep in the fish's throat. I felt I could hold the mouth open with my right hand and push my left index finger down against the third hook and back the other two hooks out of the fish's throat, doing little injury to the fish.

As my finger pushed down on the third hook the strong fish gave a violent twist. The other treble hook on the spreader was now imbedded into my left thumb past the barb. There wasn't much pain as the hook penetrated into my thumb. That quickly changed as the fish began to thrash violently driving the hook deeper into my thumb and twisting and moving the hook about. I grabbed the fish at the base of its gills with my right hand and held tight to keep it from moving its head and causing me more pain.

There I sat holding on to the fish, saying unpleasant things under my breath until the fish finally went quiet because of the lack of oxygen. It's amazing how long a fish can stay alive and thrash about after it is out of the water!

By this time the bottom of the boat was gently bumping against the shore line. There I was with a three pound dead fish attached to my hand, and a number 10 hook imbedded in my thumb well beyond the barb. I looked around. The beautiful wilderness and silence of a minute ago was now my prison. I was trapped and there was no one around to help me. So I did what any red-blooded outdoorsman would do. I put my head over the side of the boat, and relieved my stomach of its lunch.

That must have done some good because it got my mind working. I took my jack knife out of my fishing vest pocket. It is very difficult to get a jack knife open with a large fish hanging from a hook imbedded in your thumb. Next, I jammed the blade of the knife into the fish's mouth and cut loose the two imbedded hooks.

Free at last from the monster fish! He lay in the bottom of the boat—cold, slimy and dead. But there was an unmistakable gleam in its eye as it lay there looking up at me. Now, I could carefully examine the hook in my thumb without inflicting more pain. It hurt, but the adrenaline was flowing and I felt in control again.

All I had to do was just pull it out. No problem, it wasn't a big hook and it didn't have a very large barb. Taking a few deep breaths, I firmly grabbed the bend of the hook, clenched my teeth, closed my eyes, and gave the hook a sharp jerk.

The scream must have sounded like someone had killed me as it echoed and bounced off the rocky hillsides. The hook did not budge, but my head quickly went over the side of the boat, and now my breakfast had joined my lunch. Tears rolling down my eyes, teeth clenched with pain, and the acid taste of a partially digested breakfast in my mouth, I again began to survey the situation.

The jackknife caught my eye. The blade was sharp. Just one small cut into my hand along the hook and I would be free. But there is not only flesh, but tendons and blood vessels, and germs, and . . . maybe not a good idea. Besides I had suddenly decided I was not the rugged, tough outdoorsman that I had been fifteen minutes before.

It was possible to row across the lake back to my truck, drive down the mountain fifty miles to the nearest doctor or hospital and have the hook removed. A couple hundred dollars, and then drive back up the mountain, put away the boat, close the cabin, put away the gear and drive home. I had already given up a half day's work to go fishing. It was approaching sunset and the fish were just beginning to rise creating swirls on the lake's surface. The perfect conditions for fly-and-bubble fishing.

The hook in my thumb was a small hook dug into the flesh but not straight toward the bone. It was more parallel to the skin line.

Without the barb it would be no problem. Just back the hook out, suck on my thumb for a few minutes to clean the wound and continue fishing. The hook was very sharp and I barely felt it as it went in. If I could give it a quick twist I could push it and force the barb out through the surface of the skin. Then all I would have to do is remove the barb and back the hook out the same way it went in.

What did I have to lose? Last night's dinner had already passed through me. Another few deep breaths, clenching of the teeth, closed eyes, firm grip on the treble hook and a push. Just a little pain. When my eyes opened, there was the point of the hook and the barb protruding out of the skin. Now just remove the barb and I'm free to remove the hook. My kingdom for a pair of long-nosed pliers with side wire cutter. But then if I'd had those I would not have been in this predicament in the first place. What did I have? One worn out pair of fingernail clippers used to cut line and leader. The hook may have been small and thin, but the steel was hard. Very hard!

Working the clippers around the inside of the barb where the wire was the thinnest, I could finally see some progress in cutting the hook. The point with the barb attached finally broke off and I could back out the hook. I sucked the open wound until the bleeding stopped and then picked up my fly-and-bubble rod and started fishing. The lake had a slight ripple. Perfect! The sunset over the mountains was red and gold. Spectacular. The ducks were quacking in the shallows. The birds were singing their evening songs. The coyotes started howling in the distance with other coyotes answering from behind me. The fish were rolling in the water and were hungry. I thought to myself, " God, please Don't let me die. Heaven cannot be this good."

LESSON

1. Never go fishing without forceps or long-nosed pliers on your person.
2. If you find yourself in a situation where you have to reach into a fish to remove a hook, with other hooks creating a danger to you, do not try to unhook the fish with your hand. Just remove the plug from your line, leave the plug in the fish and attach another lure to your line and continue fishing.

Chapter 11

Warm Water Fish

The fishing methods described in this book were developed in fishing for the various species of trout. I have also used the fly-and-bubble method for warm water fish under many conditions. It has been used successfully on huge impoundments such as Lake Powell, small reservoirs, gravel pits, lakes of all sizes, slow moving rivers and even in the Great Lakes of the Midwest. Your success with the warm water species will depend largely on your knowledge of the specific feeding traits of the different fish. You will have to modify your presentation and choice of fly to trigger the striking mechanism of each species. Those of you who fish for a particular warm water fish in a particular lake will be best suited to make those modifications.

My experience with the various species of fish has shown the following:

A. Walleye
The walleye is a predator that loves to eat other fish. My greatest success was fishing the rocky shores of Lake Powell by gently bouncing the bubble off and between rocks along the shore. The fly was presented in a jerky, injured minnow fashion. The most productive fly was the Marabou Streamer with white marabou and silver wrapping for the body. In lakes where the minnow population is dark colored, it would seem appropriate to use brown or gray marabou to match the local bait fish.

B. Bluegill-Sunfish
The sunfish family have very small mouths and these fish tend to pick on the bait rather than strike the bait as walleye or bass would

do. Because of the small mouths on sunfish, the greatest hooking success was with small bodied flies on a #8 or #10 hook. Using an even smaller hook was productive, but many of the fish caught were very small. The slightly larger hook keeps the very small fish from getting the hook into their mouths. As the sunfish are almost always ready to eat anything placed before them, color seems to make little difference once you found the school of fish. Larger flies did receive more tugs but very few hook-ups as the fish could not get the large hook into their small mouths.

C. Crappie

In feeding habits, the crappie are somewhere between the walleye and the sunfish families. They do have relatively small mouths, but still will strike with all of the energy they possess. Small flies that represent minnows, such as the white marabou with silver bodies, Hornberg or small streamer flies will usually get strikes once the school of crappies is located. As all crappie fishermen know, depth is very important as crappies tend to suspend at a particular depth in the body of water. You must not only find the school of fish but locate the appropriate depth. At times, when the fish are no longer schooling, I have had great success fishing for crappie along the rip-rap of dams. Using the same minnow type flies, cast the bubble parallel to the dam and let it sink until it bounces on and along the rock rip-rap of the dam. The crappie would be laying along the rocks for protection and come streaking out to strike the fly going by their lair.

D. Bass

When bass fishing, it is hard to resist using top water plugs. The exhilaration that comes when a large bass smashes a top water plug throwing water for ten feet around is just too good to pass up. The long fly rod and spinning reel setup described in this book is very effective in making long casts with plugs or lures for bass fishing. In addition you have the joy of fighting a bass on a fly rod. I have tried the fly-and-bubble method on bass with very limited success. Using large minnow or leach patterns such as the Woolly Bugger has produced an occasional bass. After getting several vicious strikes and not hooking any fish, it did finally dawn on me to clip a large treble hook onto the snap swivel holding the bubble in place. To no bass fishermen's surprise, the treble hook on the bubble produced as many bass as the large fly.

E. Catfish

Catfish are scent feeders and as such, are attracted to the scent rather than the movement of the fly. I have never had success in catching catfish on a fly. The only exception was when the fly was heavily scented. My first experience with catfish on a fly was one sunny warm afternoon when I took two of my grandchildren fishing. They were quite small, three and one-half and five years old, so I tried to find a place where I was certain they would catch fish, be safe and have a good time. I selected a local reservoir that had a large population of bullheads. I knew of a slough where I was sure the bullheads would be lying on the bottom. Using night crawlers and the bubble drifting method described in Chapter 13, we quickly located the proper depth and promptly began hauling out bullheads about as fast as the night crawlers would reach the bottom.

A friend of mine came driving by to fish the same reservoir and seeing us got out and walked down to the shore to visit. He asked "Why don't you go after some of those nice little two and three pound channel cats sitting in the slough?" I looked at him and said "We'd love to hook into a two or three pound channel cat, but none of them have taken our night crawlers yet." He went back to his car and returned with his rod hooked up with a fly-and-bubble, took the fly, which was a brown woolly worm, removed a small jar from his pocket and with a stick, he pushed the fly into the brown gooey mess in the bottle. He visited a couple of minutes and then finally took the fly out of the bottle, capped the bottle tightly, stuck it back in his pocket and cast his fly where we had been catching the bullheads.

His fly could not have been on the bottom more than five to ten seconds when he was hooked into a savagely fighting fish. He promptly landed a three pound channel cat. I looked at him in amazement and asked, "How on earth did you do that?"

"Well, I just put a little stink bait on my woolly worm and those catfish don't know that it is not edible." He then explained to me that he tied his woolly worms using natural wool for the body so the material would absorb more scent. He also confessed that his little jar contained rotted, liquefied, night crawlers. He further warned that you do not let the fingers or skin touch the rotted night crawlers as they will stink to high heaven and it will take days to get the scent off of your fingers.

After catching two more nice channel cats, he left. My grandchildren and I had been fishing for about two hours on a hot sunny afternoon and our night crawler supply was getting low. The can holding the crawlers was quite warm. I tipped over the can and found a couple of partially rotted night crawlers in the bottom of the can, hooked them on to the grandchildren's lines, tossed them out and each promptly hooked into a channel cat. Both fish pulled so hard that my smallest grandchild threw down the rod and let the fish have the pole if the fish wanted the pole that badly. We ended the fishing day with two nice channel cats and a whole bucket of bullheads.

F. Carp

The carp was imported to the United States from Germany as a supreme game fish. Its American reputation is somewhat less than that. However, anyone who has ever caught a carp and felt its power and fighting ability would not deny that it is an excellent game fish. Whenever I see a school of carp feeding in the weeds or wallowing in the shallows, I quickly put on a woolly worm, soak it in fish scent, if I have any available, and with a very slow retrieve have had success at hooking these splendid fighters.

Chapter 12

Commandments of the Good Fisherman

First: *Thou shalt keep your line in the water.*

You will not catch fish while your line is out of the water. When you go fishing your equipment should be in good order. You should be prepared to fish. Standing on the shore tying knots, untangling lines, putting together rods or reels, oiling your reel, looking at the trees or the beautiful sunset will not catch a fish. Everything should be ready before you go fishing so that when you get to your location you are ready to put that fly in the water where the fish are. Even a part of the time studying a new lake as described in Chapter 7 can be done while you are fishing. Keep your line in the water!

Second: *Thou shall fish where the fish are.*

Prior to going fishing do your research on the body of water you intend to fish. Don't waste your time with unknown lakes that may have had winter kill and be completely devoid of fish. Don't go to strange places in the hope that there might be a fish in the lake. Do your checking before going fishing. Ask your friends, read sports magazines, sports pages of newspapers, or best of all, have a successful fisherman take you to his favorite lake and watch his method of fishing. You cannot catch fish where there are simply no fish to be caught. No matter how good a fisherman you are, how much you know about catching fish, how well you cast or what equipment you have, you cannot catch fish in a bathtub.

Third: *Thou shalt fish every cast like it is the perfect cast.*

As in all life's endeavors, success sometimes involves a certain amount of luck. In fishing, be positive. Assume that you are having good luck, not bad luck. So if your cast is not where you planned to place it and it falls off to the right where there could not possibly be a fish, fish that cast and work that fly as though it were the perfect cast. You can never tell where a fish is lying. There are many times when I have waded out into a lake and cast out 225 feet, only to see a large cutthroat trout feeding on minnows ten feet behind me.

Fourth: *Thou shalt check your equipment before making each cast.*

It is important that you completely check your line and equipment before making each and every cast. Make sure the line is ready to flow from the reel, that the line passes through all of the guides and is not wrapped around the rod or the top guide, that the bubble has the proper amount of water in it, and that the fly is free of all weeds or other debris.

Casting long distances requires the tip of the rod to travel at great speed. Anything that suddenly stops the free flow of the line will snap your light line and send your fly-and-bubble far into the lake. This will then require you to stop your fishing and completely redo your gear. Finding new gear and tying knots takes valuable fishing time and is a nuisance. Especially when you have fish rising in front of you and instead of being out there hooking them, you are standing on the shore threading line through guides, tying knots, looking for swivels, bubbles, leaders and flies.

I cannot say for certain that a fish will not strike a fly that has seaweed attached to it. The general feeling is that a fish will not strike a fouled hook and just to play it safe, always keep your fly-and-bubble free of all debris and in good order.

Fifth: *Thou shalt not covet another person's fishing spot.*

Sharing a smile and giving a friendly greeting to other fisherman is a sure sign that you know what you are doing. Fishing in such a way that you do not interfere with the fishing of fellow anglers or the space immediately around them is simple, common courtesy and should be observed at all times. You will find that being courteous to your fellow fisherman will not only lead to other anglers being courteous to you, but will also lead to good advice, suggestions, hints on where to fish and information as to what the fish are striking at that particular time. This can only add to your outdoor enjoyment. It costs you nothing to be courteous and friendly, but it can lead to substantial rewards.

Sixth: *Thou shall not keep more fish than you can eat in the next meal.*

Your favorite fishing spot can be fished out by **you**. Return all uninjured fish to the water so that you can have that great fishing experience again. Every fish you keep results in one less fish in the water. If you are going to eat frozen fish, buy that fish at the store. It is cheaper to do so and does not decrease the availability of fish in your favorite lake, pond or stream.

Chapter 13

Live Bait

Fishing with live bait while using a plastic bubble as a float can be extremely productive. The water in the bubble can be adjusted so that it takes very little to pull the bubble below the surface thereby giving minimal resistance to the fish. In addition, the bubble allows you to cast the bait far out into the lake where most people cannot possibly reach without using a lot of lead and going to the bottom. Painting the bubble orange or red will increase its visibility. We often repair broken bubbles with model airplane cement, fingernail polish or household cement and then paint the bubble orange to help seal the cracks. These repaired bubbles are then used to fish live bait.

To keep the line from sliding through the hole in the bubble plug you must have a swivel or snap swivel which just fits into the large hole of the bubble plug. This permits you to force the swivel loop into the bubble plug and hold your bait at the depth you wish the bait to reach. The perfect depth of the bait is just above the weed bed. See Figure 13-1, Depth of Live Bait.

If there is a breeze going across the water, the bubble will drift with the breeze thereby allowing the bait to cover a large section of water. The slight ripple action on the surface of the water causes the bait to move up and down which helps the fish see the bait and thus triggering the fish's strike mechanism. Any type of sinking bait can be used, such as worms or natural nymphs. Upon hitting the water, the bait will slowly drift down to the end of the leader in an enticing and natural manner.

If you wish to fish on the bottom of the lake you can also do that using the bubble. Simply fill the bubble with water. This will make the bubble slowly sink to the bottom since the plastic of the bubble is heavier than water. The large advantage of the plastic bubble over lead sinkers is that the bubble is heavy enough to cast a

Cast crosswind

Worm

Figure 13-1
Depth of Live Bait

long distance, but is very light under water and does not tend to hang up or get buried in the mud.

When using a sampling net to examine the lake it is wise to place any nymph, crayfish or other underwater food item in a coffee can with some water in it. Anything that is big enough to be attached to a hook will work as live bait. Everything found in the weed bed or under a log or rock will be an excellent bait for that lake. The bubble method of presenting that bait by drifting will appear very natural to the fish and can be an excellent producer.

Live minnows can be fished as other live bait by hooking the minnow in front of the dorsal fin and letting it swim naturally. The natural drift of the bubble will make certain the minnow covers a large area of the lake.

A more active method of fishing minnows, live or dead, is to rig the minnow just as you would a fly, hooking the minnow through both lips and trolling the minnow just above the weeds. There are many sinker rigs that are designed to accomplish this. Because of the buoyancy of the bubble under water, the bubble method is far superior to using lead to get the minnow down to the fish.

Casting live bait requires a more delicate casting motion than casting a fly or lure. Most bait is soft and will fall off the hook if cast with a snap. Live bait requires a *swing cast*, that is a cast where the rod tip is held behind you and from that stationary position you accelerate the tip forward with a smooth motion. See Figure 13-2 Swing Cast. Using the swing cast, the rod will still load up with energy and drive the bubble forward, but will not snap the bait off the hook. When possible, cast crosswind and let the natural drift of the float make greater coverage of the area.

Fishing live bait with small children is special. They have the excitement of watching the bubble move around and suddenly disappear. Other advantages are that the bait does not hang up on rocks and weeds as it does when fishing on the bottom of the lake.

Any movement of the bubble, as happens when an active child picks up the rod or swings it around, will probably increase the chances of getting a strike. Don't yell at the child to leave the rod alone! Just smile and let the little one have fun. This is the way a child learns to enjoy fishing and become your fishing buddy. Let

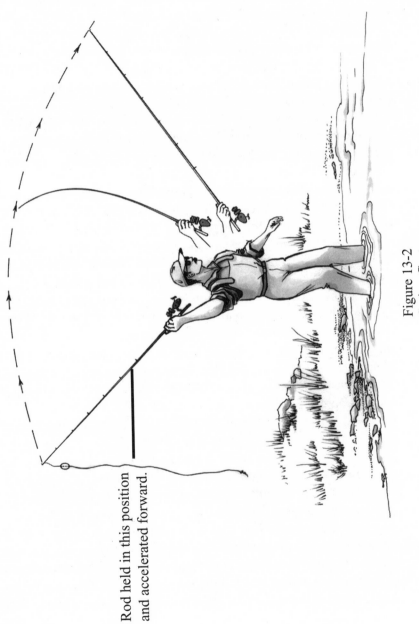

Rod held in this position
and accelerated forward.

Figure 13-2
Swing Cast

them joyfully wave the rod around and keep themselves entertained while waiting for a fish to strike.

A. Worms and Night Crawlers

The most important factor in keeping worms and night crawlers firm, fresh and lively is to keep them cool. If possible, keep them in the refrigerator but in no case let them get above 62°F as they will quickly die if they get too warm. Worms can endure more heat than night crawlers. Worms live near the surface of the ground and burrow no deeper than a few inches below the frost line.

Night crawlers normally burrow ten to twelve feet below the surface where the temperature is a steady 58°F. The crawlers come to the surface at night to cool off. This is especially true after a large amount of moisture has been placed on the surface. The cooling caused by evaporation of the water will bring the crawlers to the surface to cool off, feed and mate.

B. Worm Bedding

Garden soil and peat moss are often used for bedding of worms and night crawlers, but they are not the best bedding. The best of all bedding is soft brown corrugated cardboard. The cardboard should be broken up into pieces and soaked in water prior to placing your worms or night crawlers into the bedding. The cardboard is a clean, pleasant bedding in which the worms and night crawlers will thrive. They eat the cardboard and love the mucilage holding the corrugations and the cardboard together.

Commercial bedding as found in stores, is usually nothing more than pulverized newspapers. Shredded newspaper is an excellent bedding you can easily make by simply shredding or tearing newspapers into thin strips. Shredded newspaper is also a clean and handy bedding in which both worms and night crawlers will thrive.

Keep the bedding moist but not wet. Water in the bottom of the container will drown and kill worms and night crawlers. If a non-absorbent container is used, be certain to put drain holes in the bottom to release excess water. It is best to use one of the press-board worm containers. Evaporation through the walls of the container will help keep the worms and night crawlers cool.

C. Nymphs

It is doubtful there is a better live bait than live nymphs caught in the water where you are fishing. Sufficient nymphs to use as bait are difficult to catch and after going through all of the work of catching the nymphs, they are difficult to keep alive and active for more than a couple of hours. If you do not plan to fish again in the near future, please return any aquatic life removed from the water back into the water.

Nymphs that are large enough to put on a hook into are probably getting ready to hatch. To delay the hatching process, it is necessary to keep the nymphs in a cool dark place. A refrigerator is excellent but if you have a spouse who does not love to fish, there may be some complaints.

Nymphs breath and need oxygen. To keep a nymph healthy for any length of time, oxygen must be added to the water or the water must be changed at least once each day. Do not use tap water. The chlorine, fluorine and other chemicals placed in the water to purportedly protect you, will quickly kill the nymphs. Rain water is good if no lake water or stream water is readily available.

One of the best and most interesting ways to keep nymphs alive and healthy is to keep them in an aquarium with an aerator running. Do not use a heater. If anything, add an occasional ice cube to the water to help keep the water cool. Adding a piece of the rotted wood from the water where the nymphs were caught and a small piece of seaweed does increase the time that nymphs can be kept alive and healthy. It gives them something to hang on to, other than just each other, and if you use an aquarium, it makes an extremely interesting aquarium exhibit.

D. Crickets, Grasshoppers, Roaches and other Terrestrials

The fly-and-bubble rig will get the floating insect far out on the water where you have probably never been before except by boat. For this style of fishing use a fine wire, dry fly hook with just enough bend and gape to surround the insect. If you want to get the insect below the surface it will be necessary to use a small split shot sinker placed just above the eye of the hook. A heavier wire hook will also help pull the floating bait below the surface.

E. Minnows

Live minnows are not too sensitive to water temperature as long as there is no severe change in temperature. But remember, minnows need oxygen to survive. Either change the water frequently or if that is not possible, use an aerator. Battery powered aerators are available to transport minnows long distances.

F. Salamanders, Common Newts, Red Efts (waterdogs).

Salamanders and other lizard-like creatures are amphibians, that is, they can breathe both air and water. These small animals breed underwater and some live on land as adults, but some spend their lives underwater. They can be used as bait in both their adult and larvae stages. Their skin is smooth and soft, but all waterdogs must be kept in moist surroundings in order to live. Those caught on land can be kept healthy in a bed of moist leaves, but it is best to play it safe and keep them in well-aerated water. Too much sunlight and heat will kill all varieties.

Chapter 14

Casting Light Lures

A rod built to the specifications outlined in Chapter 17 will be a casting machine. Large plugs and lures are easily cast long distances. Small lures which normally cannot be cast with any effectiveness can be cast using a bubble with the proper amount of water and a shorter leader. The reason for the short leader is to make it easier to cast.

The weight of a lure at the end of a leader tends to produce an awkward cast if the leader is too long. The leader must just be long enough to allow the lure to maintain its complete action. See Figure 14-1, Light Lure Hookup. A wobbling lure such as a Flat Fish™ will require a leader of approximately three feet long to give it full and complete action. Other lures such as spoons will maintain their action with a leader as short as two feet. Where distance is important, using the bubble and a light lure can be effective producers.

Lake John is in North Park, Colorado. A "park" is a large valley between mountain peaks. These high altitude meadows although semiarid are fertile. When a lake is created in these parks, the lake quickly produces an abundance of fish food. The aquatic life and the fish grow fast and strong. In 1978, Lake John was one of the premier trophy fish lakes in the State of Colorado. The rolling hills surrounding Lake John are devoid of trees and brush. Just sand and sagebrush surrounded by mountains. The scenery is not what most people would call beautiful, but the fishing was sometimes spectacular. My youngest son, Greg, who had been my constant fishing and hunting companion, until he grew up, got married and moved two hundred miles away, called me in the middle of the week, "Dad, let's go fishing."

"Sure," I answered, "where and when?"

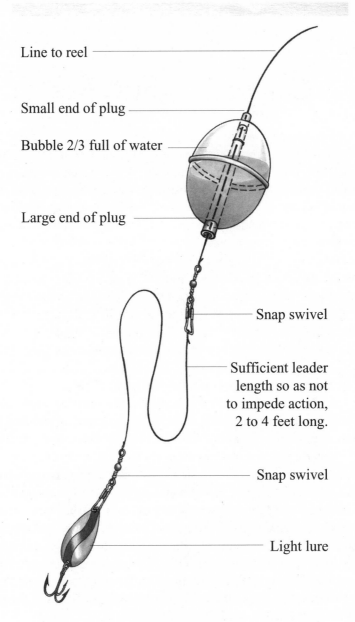

Line to reel

Small end of plug

Bubble 2/3 full of water

Large end of plug

Snap swivel

Sufficient leader length so as not to impede action, 2 to 4 feet long.

Snap swivel

Light lure

Figure 14-1
Light Lure Hookups

"Lake John this Saturday, I'll meet you there about 8 A.M."
Greg had graduated from college, had gotten married and was now
living, working and skiing in Aspen, Colorado. I left Boulder,
Colorado before daylight. I traveled up Poudre Canyon, over
Cameron Pass at daylight and arrived at Lake John about 8 A.M.
Greg was already there at our favorite spot. During the summer
months Lake John takes a lot of fishing pressure, but this was in late
September. Hunting season had started, kids were back in school and
people had other things on their minds. We had our favorite spot to
ourselves.

Our favorite spot had some problems. The weed growth was at
its highest point. Also these high lakes, under arid conditions, can
lose one-half inch of surface water per day through evaporation. It
had been a dry summer and the water level was down a foot. The sea
weed was now laying on the surface of the lake in a thick mat
extending thirty to forty feet from shore. We would have to struggle
dragging our line through those weeds with every cast.The lake
appeared dead. And, as often happens in high altitude lakes, nothing
was working.

All morning we fished, and except for the occasional boil
caused by a very large fish rolling just at the edge of the open water
past the weed bed, there was nothing to indicate that there were any
fish in this lake. We tried everything we could think of or that had
ever worked for us before at Lake John. I swept the sample net
through the weed bed and caught nymphs, crawdads and minnows
of all sizes. These we drifted just past the weed bed. Although the
one large fish continued to boil all around our bait, we had no takers.

About two in the afternoon tired, sunburnt, frustrated and bored
I decided to try fishing a lure even though taking it through the mat
of weeds would be exasperating. With a full bubble, a three foot
leader and a prayer I clipped on a slow wobbling lure about two
inches long. The first cast was allowed to sink to the count of ten.
The lake should be 10 to 12 foot deep at the point of my cast. With
a slow retrieve I could feel the lure wiggling. Three turns of the reel
and it stopped dead, hooked onto something solid.

"What the hell," I muttered under my breath, "there's no log
out there, I've fished this spot a hundred times." Nevertheless, there

I was hung up and about to lose a new $2.29 lure on the first cast. Holding the rod high and keeping some pressure on the line ,I chided myself for trying such a stupid thing as attempting to fish a lure over the top of a dense weed bed.

Standing there watching the taunt line I suddenly realized that it was slowly moving east. Snags don't usually move. Darn if I didn't have a fish. The fish never fought hard, it just seemed to bulldog and swim up and down the far edge of the weed bed. It was a long tugging match, but the fish finally tired and came to the surface. Now I had to get it across the seaweed mat. One dive into the weeds and there would be no way I could ever pull that fish out of the mat of weeds laying on the surface. Greg wadded out with the long handled landing net until the water was up to his arm pits. The fish was not flopping but just laying on the surface of the water at the edge of the weed bed.

Holding the eight foot fly rod as high as I could, I backed up with a steady gait sliding the large fish along the top of the weeds. It stated to flop attempting to dive into the weeds, but it was too late. Greg had the net under it. The six pound, twelve once brown trout now hangs on the wall of my friends cabin. The largest trout I have ever caught.

Chapter 15

Keep a Fishing Diary

A fishing diary can provide you with pleasure for life. For the first year it sometimes feels like an unwanted chore. Starting in the second year, it can only bring you pleasure. Bringing the diary up to date after each fishing trip becomes a pleasant ritual that permits reliving the events of other fishing trips. My fishing diary helps me to recall happy fishing trips that took place over more than a twenty-five year span. During this time my children grew up and I have lost track of many old fishing comrades. It is a precious record of happy and exciting times.

Whenever I review the diary I can vividly recall specific fishing trips with friends who have already passed away. Flipping through the pages of the chronicle can easily bring tears to the eyes by helping to again recall memories of things you thought you would never forget.

The first entry in my fishing diary is dated April 22, 1967 and reads as follows:

1967 Dowdy with family in afternoon.
Hatch of small gray flies @ S bay.
Rainbows raising in snowfall.
Flies good - Adams, black ant, coachman.

Just that small amount of information allows me to recall details of the trip. Fishing was just an excuse to get out into the mountains on a nice early spring afternoon. In Boulder, Colorado the weather was sunny and warm. At an altitude of 8,000 feet in the mountains it was cool with occasional snow flurries.

My oldest son was 14 years old, loved to eat fish, but did not care about fishing or the outdoors. His thing was rock music and he had just discovered girls. Because he was given no alternatives he accompanied the family to the mountains for the afternoon. Overcome by boredom and frustration he took one of the underwater scopes, put on his hip boots and proceeded to wade out into the water to see what my youngest son and I often enjoyed so much. Within minutes every preteen and early teenage girl in the campground was out there with him wanting to know what that cute guy was doing. One even waded out in the cold water in her bare feet pulling up her dress as far as she dared to keep it dry. My son discovered that there were many bored, frustrated teenage girls also out in the mountains with their families. After that trip, he gave us less trouble when required to go on future fishing trips.

My youngest son, Greg, was only seven years old and had a completely different outlook. He was already and accomplished fisherman with the fly-and-bubble. His favorite pastime was to look for some bait fisherman sitting on the shore waiting for a fish to bite. On this day he found several of them set up on a rocky point next to the bay I was fishing. Greg than violated the Fifth Commandment, elbowed his way between two of them and proceeded to fish his fly-and-bubble. The two senior citizens did not mind the little kid with the eight foot long fly rod fishing between them and were quite excited when he hooked into a nice fish. Even after having to untangle all of the lines caused by the fish running from side to side, that did not stop their good humor. They would pat Greg on the back and admire the little kid's fish before he returned it to the water.

By the forth fish much of the good humor was gone. They had not had a bite and had been regularly untangling the mess caused by the fighting fish and close quarters. About that time Greg hooked into a large fish, about a one and one-half pound rainbow that really left a mess of tangled lines. Greg unhooked the fish, held it up and shouted across the bay to me, "Dad is this one good enough to keep?" Going along with his evil little game I immediately shouted back, "No Greg, we don't keep little ones, throw it back." The old timers' who had not had a bite all this time folded up their gear and muttering something that seven-year-old Greg could not quite understand, left.

As is true of many precious things a fishing diary can cost you practically nothing. My diary is kept in a small calendar notebook that was given to me by a title insurance company. The pages are only 4 x 7 inches but that has been sufficient to contain 25 years of fishing and hunting experiences.

The diary should not be kept in chronological order, but by listing each fishing trip on the page with the correct month and day regardless of the year. In order to do this effectively, it is easiest to place your notes on a diary that has one full page for each day of the year. The information you want to keep is more relevant as to day and month than it is to the year. By this method, you can keep one book and make your report on the page for each day of the year that the trip was taken. That way, the proper sequence of fly hatches and conditions will hopefully repeat themselves in such a way that you have information you need before going fishing.

Do not carry your fishing diary with you on a fishing trip. It is easy to lose it or damage it in the rain or other bad weather. Rather, keep it in a safe place such as your desk at home or in your office. Make the entries in the diary within a day or two of each trip when all of the details are still fresh in your mind. It is amazing how facts and events you believe you could never forget are completely lost from memory within thirty days. The information that your diary should contain is as follows:

1. The date. (Year on appropriate day and month page)
2. The location of the trip with name of the lake or stream.
3. Name of persons with you on the trip.
4. Weather conditions with appropriate notations, such as "Spring was cold or late" which might have set back the normal fly hatches.
5. Notes on nymphs or fly hatches.
6. The flies, lures or bait with which you had success.
7. Your fishing results.
8. Any other data which you feel is relevant or which you think you would want to remember at a later date.

Any data that you can put into your diary can be of use to you at some future date. When talking to friends during the week who have gone fishing at a different location, I found it useful to make notes in my diary as to their trip. This information would then be

AUGUST
S	M	T	W	T	F	S
--	--	1	2	3	4	5
6	7	8	9	10	11	12
13	14	15	16	17	18	19
20	21	22	23	24	25	26
27	28	29	30	31	--	--

Saturday, AUG. 5 — Sunday, AUG. 6

1968 - Lake John w/ Greg. -
Greg got 2 about 11:30 AM
3 7/8# Brown & 4 3/8# Rainbow,
Cold front moved in.

1970 - Lost Lake - Greg & Rick Casady,
Large nymphs on hook - Kept 22
7/8# to 2 1/4# - Best clearing rain
storm at sunset. 7:00 PM.

1973 Red Rocks w/ Greg - Large
nymphs - Good on F-Lye Adams
and Little green fly.

1978 - Dowdy w/ Greg - poor
Parvin Lake poor until evening
rise - Bk Wooly Worm and
nymph.

1978 - Caney Lake w/ Greg & Zack -
Storm moved over at sunset.
1 good cutthroat on #8 Adams.
Long slender, tan nymphs on rocks

1984 - Sunset Lake - Best Fishing
7:30 - 8:30 PM best on
ring worms.

DAILY EXPENSES	CAR (MILEAGE)	FARES
MEALS	HOTEL	PHONE
TIPS	ENTERTAINMENT	MISC.

Figure 15-1, Fishing Diary

Monday, AUGUST 7, 1967

SEPTEMBER
S M T W T F S
1 2
3 4 5 6 7 8 9
10 11 12 13 14 15 16
17 18 19 20 21 22 23
24 25 26 27 28 29 30

1967 - Long Lake w/ Greg & Sparkie,
Calm at sunset - 7 good Brook
w/ #14 Royal Coachman

1971 - Creedmore w/ Greg -
Damsel Fly hatch. - Nymph
and little green Fly - 3 - 2# and
many more

1980 - Moreene Lake w/ Greg.
Evening rise - little green fly,
nymph, wooley worm

1982 - Berthoud Lake w/ Cal
and Sten - 8 crappie on
white Marabou - 3 rainbow
on Hornberg

1985 - Cowdry Lake w/ Mel
5:30 P.M. fishing started.
Algee on lake, best adjacent
to boat ramp. Lures best

1988 - Erie w/ Arden, Mel +
Elenore, Yellow flatfish,
panter marten - Flies - Royal
Coachman best.

DAILY EXPENSES CAR (MILEAGE)_____FARES_____
MEALS_____HOTEL_____PHONE_____
TIPS_____ENTERTAINMENT_____MISC._____

Figure 15-1, Fishing Diary

used in later years when I would take a trip to the same area at approximately the same time of year.

After the first year you will find yourself referring to your diary prior to each fishing trip. Review the notes of previous years for the two weeks before the date of your next trip and for the two week period after the planned trip. This gives information about fly hatches, weather conditions, successful flies or lures and successful fishing methods. Of course the longer you keep the notes, the more data you have.

A copy of a couple pages of my fishing diary are reproduced in Figure 15-1. Reviewing those notes show that on July 4, 1967 my then seven-year-old son and I hiked the three miles to Lost Lake with my old friend Dick Sparks. Even though I have lost track of Dick for the last fifteen years, those notes return to me memories of that first trip to Lost Lake.

Chapter 16

Smoking and Canning Fish

World-wide the water and fishing resources are diminishing while the human population is increasing. Under these circumstances, it is only logical to preserve these sport fishing resources. To do this as many fish as possible should be returned to the water unharmed. Returning uninjured fish to the water will help sustain the quality of fishing and especially preserve the quality of your fishing in the place where you like to fish. An injured fish will only die and therefore should not be returned to the water.

The key to your present and future fishing experience is conservation, not preservation. Utilizing and eating an injured fish is an appropriate conservation measure and does no harm to the fishery. As a rule of thumb, any fish that is bleeding is definitely injured and will probably die. Taking fish home to freeze for future consumption is counterproductive and injurious to your fishing experience. If you are going to eat frozen fish it would seem that it would be more logical to purchase the frozen fish at the grocery store. To preserve your future fishing experience, return to the water those fish caught at your favorite lake for future enjoyment. You cannot economically justify keeping fish for future consumption. Purchasing the same fish at the supermarket is probably one-tenth the cost of going fishing and catching the fish yourself.

There are times when you would like to preserve the fish for future use and enjoyment especially when you have more injured fish in your possession than you can consume immediately. If you are going to preserve fish for future consumption, two of the best methods of preservation are smoking and canning. Both offer good preservation for future use along with new and exotic flavors for your enjoyment.

A. Smoking Fish

Smoking methods using the compact commercially made smoking units makes smoking fish convenient and easy. If you wish to build a smoker, numerous magazine articles describe different methods of constructing a smoker. These methods range from the digging of pits in the ground to using old refrigerators. In my opinion, nothing beats the new modern smokers that not only do a good job in a short time, but they are also attractive units so that your spouse or neighbors do not object to the smoker sitting in your back yard or patio.

Two factors control the flavor of the fish during the smoking process. They are: (1) the wood and (2) the brine.

1. Wood

Hickory was the old standby for all smoking chores and it is certainly one of the best woods to use. To give the fish a different flavor use any wood from any fruit tree. If you have a fruit tree in your yard such as apple, cherry, peach, plum or pear, use the trimmings from that tree to add a very pleasant and delicate flavor to the fish. Mesquite is also a popular flavor for smoking and is readily available at most stores.

Experimenting with the type of wood to change the flavor of the fish is one of the more enjoyable experiences in the smoking process. Regardless of what wood is used, it is necessary to soak the wood in water for at least eight hours prior to starting the smoking process. This permits the wood to smolder rather then burn and provides the smooth flavor which good smoked fish should possess.

2. Brine

The major elements in the brining process are salt and water. The fish should be soaked in the brine for eight to twelve hours before smoking. The brining process allows the flavor of the brine to permeate the fish. The old rule of thumb on the amount of salt to use is to add enough salt so that an egg will float in the brine. With people now attempting to use less salt in their diet, many of the modern brines call for less salt. Less than approximately one cup of salt per gallon of water is not advisable as the salt also helps sanitize and preserves the fish through the process of oxidation.

Other additions to the brine can be selected to suit your personal taste. Garlic, lemon, brown sugar, and any of a wide variety of spices such as bay leaf, oregano or other spices will each change the flavor.

When brining the fish, keep the brine and the fish cool by keeping them in a refrigerator or covered with an ice pack. The fish should be completely submerged in the cold brine for the whole brining process.

3. Smoking Time

The length of time it takes to smoke the fish varies with the thickness of the fish and the temperature of the smoker. Using the new commercial smokers with a water pan below the fish provides for hot-smoking, that is, smoking at a temperature higher than 85 degrees Fahrenheit. At that temperature you can adequately smoke fish up to two inches in thickness in about two hours. The longer the fish is smoked the drier it becomes. It is a matter of taste as to how long you should smoke a particular fish.

My Favorite Smoked Trout Recipe:

> 8 fish (12-14 inches long without heads)
> 2 quarts water (need enough to completely submerge fish)
> One cup canning salt
> 3 garlic sections (crushed)
> 1/2 cup brown sugar
> Juice of 1/2 lemon
> 1/4 teaspoon oregano or other spice to suit your taste (crush by placing in palm of hands and rubbing palms together to release flavor).
> Soak in brine overnight, or no less than six hours.
> Smoke 1 1/2 to 2 hours at 100 degrees Fahrenheit.

B. Canning Fish

Canning is an old and tried method of processing and preserving fish for future use. Because of contamination from bacteria and other organisms, it is highly recommended that a pressure cooker be used in home canning. The pressure cooker permits the canning process to take place at a much higher temperature than by merely boiling. The high temperature destroys more bacterial contamination in the fish. The instruction manual that comes with a pressure cooker details the method of canning that is to be used with that particular pressure cooker. One advantage of canning fish is that it permits the bones to remain in the fish and be consumed. Eating the fish bones provides the body with additional calcium. There are many recipes for canning. Experiment to find one you like.

Wide mouth pint size jars make packing the fish easier and the pint size is an adequate amount of fish for most family uses. Using pint size wide mouth jars, skin the fish and cut the fish to a length of two inches below the top of the jar. Pack the jar loosely with fish.

One of my favorite recipes is to add:
1 tablespoon of western dressing (any oil based dressing such as Italian will also do)
1 tablespoon of white vinegar (some people prefer wine vinegar). The addition of the small amount of salad dressing and vinegar will give your fish a zesty flavor and subdue the fishy taste that some people find offensive.
1/2 teaspoon canning salt.
Place in pressure cooker and cook in accordance with the instruction contained with the pressure canning unit.

Chapter 17

Building The Rod

Building a custom rod for fly-and-bubble fishing is a wonderful project for those long winter months when you can't fish but still have daydreams of the fishing season to come. The following is a step-by-step procedure which should allow you to build, with a little bit of time, a little bit of money, and great satisfaction, the perfect rod for fly-and-bubble fishing.

To make certain these steps are clear and complete, an inexperienced fisherman (the editor) was provided this chapter and actually built a rod specifically designed for fly-and-bubble fishing. Whenever he got confused or did not understand a portion of the instructions, the instructions were rewritten in a manner that hopefully made them clear. If you do have problems building the rod, most public libraries have several good books on rod building. Good luck and happy winding.

Figure 17-1. List of Materials

a. Rod blank (7 foot to 9 foot in length)
b. Fly rod reel seat
c. Fly rod handle (cork or foam)
d. Set of matched Ferrules
e. Top Guide (ceramic)
f. Guides (Set of 6 or 7 ceramic guides plus one 30mm guide)
g. Masking tape
h. Cork tape
i. Soft ferrule cement, epoxy glue or other waterproofing bonding agent such as Pliobond
j. Stick ferrule cement
k. Winding thread (size A, in your choice of color)

l.   Color preservative

m. Rod varnish or other finish material

n.   Steel wool (fine and medium)

o.   Candle

p.   Matches

q.   Sandpaper

Figure 17-2. List of Tools

a.   Long-nosed pliers

b.   Pen knife

c.   Measuring tape and ruler

d.   Rat tail files

e.   Wood rasp

f.   Sharpening stone

g.   Small artist brush

h.   Clean, lint free rag.

i.   Felt-tip marking pen.

A. Examining A Used Rod or New Rod Blank
1. Used Fly Rod Blank.

A used fiberglass fly rod can easily and inexpensively be obtained at a flea market or garage sale for five to ten dollars. A new rod blank can be purchased from some fly fishing shops and many of the mail order fishing supply companies. Many of these companies advertise in the classified section of fishing and other sporting magazines.

The older fiberglass rod blanks have the slow, soft action which is what you are looking for. Any snap in the cast can break off the bubble and all of the other equipment you are attempting to cast. A nice, slow, easy bend that will slowly accelerate and drive the bubble a long distance with little effort is wanted.

When shopping for a suitable used rod you want a rod with a good reel seat of sufficient length to mount the spinning reel. The rest of the rod hardware is of no use and should be replaced. If the handle is damaged it is easily replaced with a new handle available through many sporting goods stores and fishing supply catalogs. The top guide should be replaced with an appropriate size ceramic top guide and all the snake guides will be replaced with ceramic guides. Double-footed guides work just fine, but tend to stiffen the action of the rod slightly. For that reason I prefer the single-footed ceramic guides.

a. Reel Seat

Carefully examine the fly rod reel seat to determine its condition. If it is scraped up, bent or otherwise in poor condition, it is advisable to purchase a new reel seat for a few dollars to justify the time investment in rebuilding the rod. Mount your spinning reel onto the reel seat to see if it holds the reel firmly and is the proper size to fit your spinning reel. If the used rod has a good quality reel seat but the base of your reel is too long and will not fit into the reel seat, it is possible to file down the spinning reel base to fit the reel seat.

With the spinning reel firmly mounted on the reel seat, put pressure on the reel in all directions to make certain that the reel seat is rigid. If the reel seat is loose it should be glued or replaced as described in Section 2, New Rod Blank. The reel seat is mounted so that the spinning reel is at the very end of the rod. See Figure 17-3, Reel Seat and Handle.

b. Cork Handle

Examine the condition and feel of the handle of the rod. If it is in good condition and the proper size and shape for your hand, there is no reason why it cannot be left in place. A handle built up of cork cylinders can be repaired as described under Section **B.2.**, Handle or Grip. A solid cork handle or composition handle that is damaged should be removed and replaced with a new handle of your choice. See Figure 17-3, Reel Seat and Handle.

c. Metal Ferrules

The ferrules are the part of the rod that connect the sections together. The condition of the metal ferrules should be carefully examined. If they are dented, damaged, fit too loose or too tight they should be removed and replaced as described in the Section **B.3.**, Ferrules on page 150.

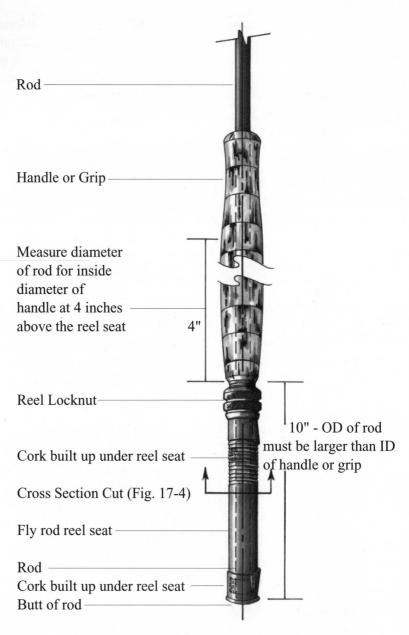

Rod

Handle or Grip

Measure diameter
of rod for inside
diameter of
handle at 4 inches
above the reel seat

4"

Reel Locknut

10" - OD of rod
must be larger than ID
of handle or grip

Cork built up under reel seat

Cross Section Cut (Fig. 17-4)

Fly rod reel seat

Rod
Cork built up under reel seat
Butt of rod

Figure 17-3
Reel Seat and Handle

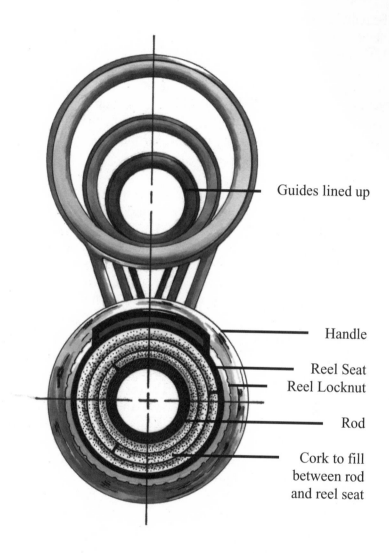

Guides lined up

Handle

Reel Seat
Reel Locknut

Rod

Cork to fill
between rod
and reel seat

Figure 17-4
Rod Cross Section

Metal Ferrules are sold in matched sets and both ferrules must be removed and replaced. Both ends of the rod must be measured to determine the proper ferrule size. See Figure 17-5, Matched Ferrules. If the rod has a built-in ferrule plug and the ferrule is loose, the male end of the plug can be coated with a layer of clear hard nail polish to provide a tighter fit. Another method of tightening the built-in ferrule is to gently sand or grind down the opening of the female end. This will decrease the hole diameter making the fit tighter. It is also advisable to wind a layer of thread over the female end to tighten and strengthen that portion of the rod.

d. Top Guide

The fly rod top guide will have to be removed by heating it over a candle. CAUTION: Overheating the guide will damage the tip of the rod. Do not hold the top guide over a flame longer than three seconds, rolling it all the while, so as to disperse the heat. After heating do not touch the top guide with your fingers as it will be very hot. Remove it with long-nosed pliers. If after two or three seconds of heating, the top guide does not remove easily, then repeat the process in two second increments until it does slip off. It should require almost no effort to remove the top guide after the glue has softened.

e. Guides

The fly rod snake guides should be carefully removed by using a pen knife to cut the thread or tape in the vacant area between the foot of the guide and the rod. Take care not to cut the rod surface with the blade. Breaking the resin surface of the rod can weaken the rod. The thread can then be removed without damaging the surface of the rod by simply peeling the thread off the rod with the fingernail. Any nick in the rod surface will create a weak point that can cause the rod to rupture under stress.

2. New Rod Blank

Carefully measure the rod blank in the areas stated below so that you can order the appropriate size materials and components to complete the rod.

a. Reel Seat

Measure the outside diameter (OD) of the butt of the rod to determine the inside diameter (ID) of the new reel seat. You should not order a reel seat with an inside diameter (ID) smaller than the exterior butt diameter (OD) of the rod. Normally, the reel seat will have a inside diameter (ID) substantially larger than the outside diameter (OD) of the rod. This will require the butt end of the rod to be built up with cork tape to provide a tight fit for the reel seat.

b. Handle

Measure the outside diameter (OD) of the rod approximately ten inches forward of the back end of the reel seat or butt of the rod. See Figure 17-3. This will determine the inside diameter (ID) of your new handle. The inside diameter (ID) of the new handle should be no more than the outside diameter (OD) of the rod at that point. To obtain a tight fitting handle you will have to remove some of the material from the inside of the handles. See Figures 17-3 and 17-4.

c. Ferrules

If new ferrules are required, measure both ends of the rod where they meet. Matched ferrules are usually two diameters. By that is meant that one end has a larger inside diameter than the other end. The upper end, or smaller end of the rod, can be sanded a small amount to allow the ferrule to fit snug. The outside diameter (OD) of the larger end or lower or butt portion of the rod should be smaller than the inside diameter (ID) of the larger ferrule. The butt end of the rod should not be sanded or made smaller by any method.

Butt portion of rod   Female half of ferrule
on butt portion of rod

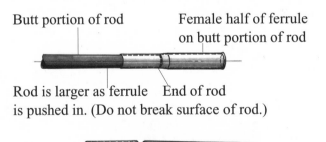

Rod is larger as ferrule   End of rod
is pushed in. (Do not break surface of rod.)

Male half of ferrule   Trim edges to get snug fit. Rod
gets smaller as ferrule is pushed
on. Insert to end of ferrule.

Figure 17-5
Matched ferrules

Removing or damaging the surface resin of the rod will greatly weaken the rod at that point and can cause the rod to rupture. See Figure 17-5, Matched Ferrules.

Ferrules are sized in 1/64ths of an inch. If unsure of the size, order an additional set a size larger and an additional set a size smaller than you believe you need. The unused ferrules can be returned.

d. Top Guide

The tip diameter of the rod is measured one-half inch below the top of the rod to determine the rod's outside diameter (OD). This outside diameter (OD) of the rod tip is the same as the inside diameter (ID) size of the top guide.

Top guides sizes are stated in numbers designating the inside diameter (ID) of the guide in increments of 1/64 of an inch. Half numbers (.5) are used to indicate 1/128 of an inch. The tip of the rod should fit snugly into the top guide. If unsure of the size, e.g., a #6 is 6/64ths ID, it is better to order a top guide that is a half-size larger, i.e. #6.5 (13/128ths). Any looseness will be filled with stick ferrule cement. Do not break the surface of the tip of the rod blank as that is the weakest point on the rod. Any damage to the surface resin will weaken the rod and cause the tip to rupture.

B. Building the Rod
READ EACH SECTION COMPLETELY BEFORE STARTING WORK!

1. Reel Seat
a. Used Rod

If the reel seat is damaged or in bad condition, it should be replaced with a new reel seat as described in **b.** on page 147. If the reel seat is in good condition but loose, it can be removed by placing the rod with reel seat attached in boiling water until hot, and then firmly pulling the reel seat off of the rod. This is the one area of the rod where a moderate amount of twisting is permissible. If the boiling water does not remove the reel seat, it may be necessary to remove the handle in order to get the water to penetrate the glue attaching the reel seat. As a last resort the reel seat can be heated by direct flame as previously described to remove the top guide. The used reel seat can then be reinstalled in the same manner as a new reel seat discussed in **b.** below.

b. Reel Seat Installation

DO NOT HURRY. A custom built rod is a thing of beauty and the small amount of time it takes to do it right is well worth the investment.

1) Purchase a new reel seat with an inside diameter (ID) larger than the outside diameter (OD) of the butt of the rod.

2) The butt of the rod will have to be built up under both ends of the reel seat with cork tape so that the reel seat has a firm foundation upon which to sit.

3) Build up the butt end of the rod to fit the reel seat by wrapping layers of cork tape at the butt end. Butt joint each layer. Leave enough room at the end of the rod for a reel seat plug if required. NOTE: Do not overlap the cork tape, as that will cause the build up section of the rod to be out of round. If the cork tape does not have an adhesive on it, it can be secured by soft ferrule cement or other adhesive. The ends of each layer of cork do not have to butt together perfectly, but they should be close.

4) Add layers of cork tape staggering the butted ends at each layer until the outside diameter (OD) of the last layer is slightly larger than the inside diameter (ID) of the reel seat. Using fine sandpaper, the last layer of the cork tape can be sanded until the reel seat has a snug fit. Repeat this procedure at the forward end of the reel seat.

5) By reversing the reel seat and placing it over the top end of the lower portion of the rod, the cork tape can be accurately measured and sanded down until the front of the reel seat has a snug fit against the cork.

6) Before attaching the reel seat to the cork base it will be necessary to roll the rod to determine the location of the hard spot or spline on the rod. A fiberglass rod will not flex evenly in all directions. One position of the rod is stiffer. This line of stiffness must be located and the guides, top guide and reel seat aligned along the spline so that the rod will cast true.

One method of locating the hard spot or spline is by leaning the rod between the floor and a wall at an approximately 45 degree angle. Then roll the rod across your fingers and against the wall. As the rod rolls you will notice that there is a hard spot on the rod. This spot should be marked with a marking pen as a line upon which to place the guides and the top of the reel seat. If you cannot find a hard spot on the lower portion of the rod, it may be too slight to be of importance and therefore can be ignored. See Figure 17-6, Finding the Hard Spot or Spline on page 154.

Another method of finding the spline or hard spot is to balance the rod section on a Stryofoam cup. The rod will roll by itself placing the heaviest portion of the rod on the bottom. The heaviest portion of the rod will be the spline.

7) Be sure to mount the reel seat so that the reel is placed at the butt end of the rod. See Figure 17-3, Reel Seat and Handle.

8) The reel seat can now be mounted to the rod with soft ferrule cement or other adhesive. Remember the reel should mount at the very back or butt of the rod. The wet cement will act as a lubricant and allow adjustments with little effort. The reel retaining portion of the reel seat must be in line with the hard spot or spline of the rod. It will take a day or two for the ferrule cement to harden completely, but if you work gently you can continue to work on the rod prior to the ferrule cement hardening.

2. Handle or Grip

In order to adjust the location of your hand when casting and to provide the best balance, it is an advantage to have a longer than normal handle length. Normal cork and composition handles are six inches long. Handles build out of cork rings can be extended to any length by simply adding more cork rings. The longer grip will not change the action of the fly rod. Two or three inches added to the grip length should be sufficient.

a. Determining the Inside Diameter of the Handle

Order a handle whose inside hole diameter (ID) is slightly less than the outside diameter (OD) of the rod measured at the end of the reel seat. See Figure 17-3, Reel Seat and Handle. Enlarge the inside diameter of the handle so it fits snug. If cork rings are used it may be necessary to order two sets of cork rings. One set of cork rings whose inside diameter (ID) is slightly less than the outside diameter (OD) of the rod at the forward end of the reel seat, and another set of cork rings whose inside diameter (ID) is slightly smaller than the rod outside diameter (OD) approximately six inches forward of the reel seat.

The necessity of ordering two separate sets of cork rings will depend upon the taper of the rod and the amount of sanding or filing you are willing to do. If the taper of the rod makes the outside diameter of the rod smaller than the inside diameter (ID) of the cork rings, the fit will not be tight. In this situation, the next smaller inside diameter (ID) cork ring should be ordered to make sure each cork ring has a good snug fit.

b. Used Rod Handle

1) The end portions of a cork ring handle on a used rod can be repaired by using new cork cylinders. In repairing the handle in the area adjacent to the reel seat, carefully remove each damaged cork ring with a pen knife. Then using steel wool, clean the rod area underneath of all debris and glue.

Using cork rings of the proper hole size, cut each ring in half with a pen knife and remove the excess cork from the inside of the ring until each ring fits snugly around the rod and the ring has a snug fit at the cut. The cork ring can then be glued in place with liquid ferrule cement or other waterproof adhesive. Remember to place the adhesive not only on the rod but on the cuts of the rings and on the faces of the rings where the cork rings touch all adjacent cork ring faces.

2) To replace damaged cork rings on the front end of the handle, again carefully remove the damaged ring with a pen knife and clean the rod of all debris and glue using steel wool.

3) Slip the new cork rings over the top of the rod and slide each ring down to the cork handle. You will likely have to remove some cork from the hole of each cork ring to make the ring fit snugly against the rod. The cork rings can be set in place by ferrule cement or other waterproof adhesive. Be sure to cement not only the cork ring to the rod but also to the sides of the adjacent cork rings where they contact each other.

4) After the cement holding the new cork rings has completely hardened, a wood rasp can be used to rough shape the handle. Final smooth shaping of the handle can be done with fine steel wool or sandpaper. End the shaping process by working over both the new

and the old cork with steel wool until the whole handle looks clean and new. If it is decided to completely replace the handle, then follow the procedure below.

c. New Rod Handle

1) First, determine whether you prefer a handle of cork or composition. If you decide on cork, you must then decide whether you wish to use a one piece cork handle or a handle made of cork rings glued together and shaped to fit your hand.

2) The selected handle is placed at the top of the lower rod section and slid down the rod. Take careful note of where the handle first binds. Remove the handle and using a round rat-tail file slowly work away that area of the handle that binds until the handle butts against the reel seat with a snug fit.

3) push the handle forward and clean the rod with a damp rag. When the rod is dry, apply soft ferrule cement or other waterproof adhesive to the rod and slip the handle in place. The glue will act as a lubricant and the handle can be twisted to spread the adhesive evenly.

4) If cork rings are chosen for the new handle they can be fitted, one ring at a time as described in **2.b.2**), page 149. Work away excess material from the inside diameter of each cork ring using the rat-tail file. Glue each ring not only to the rod, but cover the sides of each ring with adhesive where the rings touch each other. Gently twisting each ring while the adhesive is still liquid will help evenly spread the adhesive. Add rings until the desired length is reached.

5) After the glue has dried sufficiently, the cork can be rough-shaped to fit your hand using a wood rasp. Use fine steel wool or sandpaper to finish.

3. Ferrules

a. Used Rod

One of the most frustrating problems in fishing is having rod ferrules that do not join firmly or are loose. Always lubricate the male ferrule before joining the two parts of the rod. One of the best lubricants for ferrules is the face oil just below your ear at the back of your cheek or at the side of your nose. Rubbing the ferrule on one of those spots prior to each rod assembly will aid in disassembly later. See Figure 8-1, Lubricating the Ferrule.

The ferrule should fit snug. At the same time you should be able to separate the rod sections without excessive pulling or twisting. If the rod has a built-in plug style ferrule and it is looser than it should be, it can sometimes be tightened by gently sanding the face of the butt end of the female ferrule. This will reduce the inside diameter of the female ferrule. Sand down the face of the opening until a snug fit is accomplished. A wrapping of thread over the female end of the ferrule can add to its strength, serviceability and sometimes tighten the ferrule.

1) To remove old metal ferrules, it is necessary to heat the ferrule to a temperature sufficient to melt the solid ferrule cement attaching the ferrule to the rod. CAUTION: Overheating of the ferrule may damage your rod. Always follow the procedure described below.

2) Using a candle, the ferrule metal can be heated by rotating the ferrule over the flame for no more than three seconds. (That is counting: one and one thousand, two and one thousand, three and one thousand) CAUTION: Do not touch the metal ferrule with your fingers as it can become extremely hot and cause a severe burn.

3) After heating the ferrule by rotating it over the flame, grasp the ferrule with long nosed pliers and give it a firm pull. If the ferrule does not come loose, then repeat the process of heating the ferrule over the flame for no more than two seconds at a time. The ferrule will eventually come loose and after the rod has cooled, clean the area of the rod where the ferrule was attached with fine steel wool.

b. Attaching New Ferrules

1) Female ferrule

a) The female ferrule is attached to the lower or butt end of the rod.

b) Taking your matched two diameter set of ferrules, place the larger inside diameter end of the female ferrule on the top of the lower or butt half of the rod. If the ferrule opening does not quite fit over the top of the butt end of the rod, the ferrule is too small. **Do not remove any material from the rod surface.** *Breaking the resin surface will weaken the rod. You must use a larger ferrule.*

The outside diameter (OD) of the butt half of the rod increases as the ferrule slips down the rod, therefore the female portion of the ferrule should slip over the top of the lower or butt half of the rod without difficulty. See Figure 17-5, Matched Ferrules. The end of the rod should slide into the ferrule a sufficient distance to provide a firm connection.

c) Lay the ferrule next to the rod and mark the point where the end of the rod should stop inside the ferrule. That is the point where the ferrule necks down to a smaller diameter. See Figure 17-5, Matched Ferrules. Do not sand on the rod surface to make the ferrule fit. Sanding can break through the resin finish of the rod and seriously jeopardize the strength of the rod.

d) The ferrule is held in place by solid ferrule cement. Soften the stick ferrule cement by holding the ferrule cement stick over a candle flame until it is soft.

e) When the cement is soft, rub some of the soft ferrule cement on the rod sides from the end of the rod to approximately one-half inch short of the mark made in **c)** above.

f) Holding the ferrule with pliers over the flame, heat the large end of the female ferrule. The large end of the female ferrule must be heated to a point where it will melt the ferrule cement. Use enough ferrule cement to fill in any void between the ferrule and the rod.

g) The temperature of the female ferrule can be tested by touching the heated ferrule to the ferrule cement. If hot enough the ferrule cement will soften again.

h) With pliers, gently hold the ferrule so as not to deform the metal. Push the smaller diameter end of the hot ferrule over the end of the rod until it stops or reaches the mark made in **c)** above. The heated ferrule will melt the ferrule cement as it slides down the rod and will form a good seal. While the ferrule is still hot you can gently rotate the ferrule to improve the seal. If, after cooling, the ferrule is not firmly held to the rod, the ferrule can be heated while still on the rod for three seconds and then allowed to cool again. Test again to make certain the ferrule is tight to the rod. It may be necessary to repeat the whole procedure again and add more ferrule cement in order to get a good bond.

i) After the ferrule has cooled, any excess cement extending past the ferrule can be chipped off with a pen knife. Be careful not to nick the surface of the rod. The ferrule surface can be cleaned with almost any household cleaner.

2) Male Ferrule

a) The male ferrule is attached to the bottom of the top portion of the rod.

b) To attach the male ferrule to the upper portion of the rod, you must remember that at the bottom of the upper rod section tapers towards the tip of the rod, starting off thicker and then getting thinner.

c) Under these circumstances you can slightly sand down the base of the top half of the rod so that the rod fits snugly into the male ferrule. The end of the rod should reach to the bottom of the male ferrule.

d) Repeat the attachment described in **b.1) d)** to **b.1) i)** above.

4. Cleaning the Rod Surface

Gently clean the full rod surface using very fine steel wool. Be extremely careful not to penetrate the resin holding the fiberglass rod together. You just want to remove dirt, film and smooth the rough spots. The new finish will correct many of the imperfections.

5. Rolling the Rod

a. Before attaching the top guide to the tip of the rod with ferrule cement it is necessary to roll the upper section of the rod to determine its hard spot or spline.

b. First, strip the rod of all guides including the top guide.

c. Second, place the rod section at about a 45 degree angle against a wall.

d. Third, gently pushing your finger and hand across the rod and roll the rod between the floor and wall. See Figure 17-6, Finding the Hard Spot or Spine. You can also use the Stryofoam cup method described earlier. Notice that the rod has a hard spot. This is the spot where the rod tends to flex the least and it should be quite noticeable. It is along the hard spot or spline of the rod that the guides are placed. Align the guides

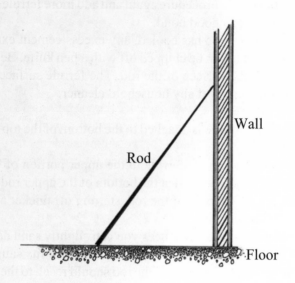

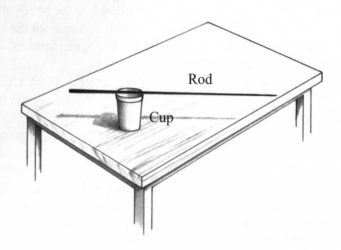

Figure 17-6
Finding the Hard Spot or Spline

with the top guide. If you do not place the guides along that line, the rod will tend to cast to the side, and when an accurate cast is necessary, it will be more difficult to accomplish. The hard spot or spline can be marked with a small touch of a felt-tip marking pen.

6. Top Guide

a. Measure the outside diameter of the rod one-half inch below the tip of the rod. That point will provide the outside diameter (OD) of the rod tip which is the same as the inside diameter (ID) of top guide ferrule. The top guide is purchased in inside diameter increments of 1/64 of an inch. In the event the hole of the top guide purchased does not freely fit over the tip of the rod, do not sand or decrease the outside surface of the rod tip. Purchase a larger top guide. It is better to have a slightly larger top guide than weaken the tip of the rod by breaking the resin surfaces. The ferrule cement will fill the top guide ferrule and give the top guide a firm fit.

b. Use hard ferrule cement to mount the top guide.

c. Use the same procedure of heating and cementing as described in the attachment of ferrules. See Section **3.b.**, page 151.

d. The top guide should be aligned with the hard spot on the rod. Minor adjustments in alignment can be made, after the top guide has cooled and the cement has hardened, by reheating the top guide ferrule to soften the ferrule cement. CAUTION: Do not overheat the tip of the rod as it will weaken the rod tip and may cause the tip of the rod to break when placed under stress.

7. Guides

To obtain maximum distance, the placement of the first and largest ceramic guide is of the utmost importance. The first guide should be a 30mm guide mounted at a point which is one-third of the length of the rod measured from the butt of the rod. See Figure 17-8, Wrapping the Guides. This allows the coils of line leaving the reel to be condensed with the least amount of friction. Friction will cause loss of casting distance. The other guides should be located as shown in Figure 17-7, Guide Spacing Chart.

NOTE: The Guide Spacing Chart shows the guides evenly spaced. The guides are spaced in increments as indicated by the numbers and not evenly spaced.

Seven guides are adequate for an 8 ft. rod but longer rods require an additional guide for proper rod action and line flow.

a. Size of Guides

Purchase a set of five or six light weight ceramic guides. In addition you will need one 30mm guide. In the event your rod requires one or two additional guides, purchase the next largest guide that is not included in the set. This will taper down the spiraling line with the least amount of friction and provide the maximum casting distance.

b. One or Two Footed Guides.

Two footed guides can be attached by narrow plastic tape available from sporting goods stores and fishing supply catalogs. It is better to wrap the guides with thread. The use of plastic tape to attach the one footed guides is not recommended. A diagram illustrating a normal thread wrapping procedure is shown in Figure 17-8, Wrapping the Guides

c. Wrapping the Guides.

1) Before placing each guide on the rod, gently grind the bottom of the foot of the each guide with a sharpening stone until the foot of each guide sits flat against the rod and is free of burrs. Then, grind the top end of the foot of each guide to a point so that the winding thread can neatly work its way up the foot of each guide.

2) Locate the 30mm guide one-third of the distance from the butt of the rod. See Figure 17-7, Guide Spacing Chart and Figure 17-8, Wrapping the Guides.

3) The 30mm guide should be mounted along the hard spot or spline of the butt half of the rod and in line with the reel sleeve on the reel seat.

4) Mount the top half of the rod on a table by placing masking tape over the male ferrule with the hard spot or spline on top. The top guide should also be perpendicular to the table and can be held down with a piece of masking tape to ensure the stability of the rod.

5) Measure the location of each guide and mark the location of each guide on the rod as shown in Figure 17-7, Guide Spacing Chart.

GUIDE SPACING CHART

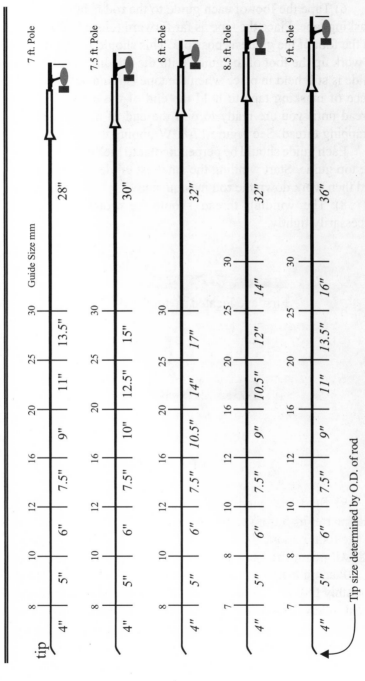

Figure 17-7
Guide Spacing Chart

6) Tape the foot of each guide to the rod using a thin piece of masking tape. Place the tape as far forward (close to the guide ring) on the foot of the guide as possible. This should leave enough room to work up the foot of the guide with the winding thread so that the guide is still held in place when the tape is removed. You can use a piece of masking tape to hold the end of the looped pull-through thread until you are ready to pull the end of the thread under the wrapping thread. See Figure 17-8, Wrapping the Guides

Each guide should be perpendicular to the table and in line with the top guide. Start winding the smallest guide at the tip of the rod and then work down the rod in sequence.

8) The winding thread should be wound firmly but not necessarily tightly.

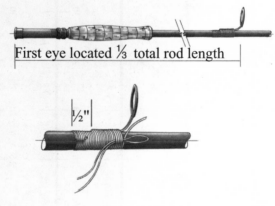

First eye located ⅓ total rod length

Figure 17-8
Wrapping the Guides

9) Start the wind of the thread approximately one-half to one-quarter inch from the end of each foot of the guide. As you work up the foot, remove the tape and close off as shown in Figure 17-8.

8. Aligning the Guides

Placing the guides in perfect alignment allows the line to flow smoothly through the guides with the least amount of friction. This is extremely important. Adjusting the alignment of the guides is possible without unwinding the thread or loosening the guides by the following procedure:

a. Join the rods together at the ferrules.

b. Hold the rod so that the eyes are standing up. See Figure 17-9, Aligning the Guides.

c. From the butt of the rod sight down the line of guides.

d. The reel seat and the 30mm guide should line up with the top guide and all guides in between should be in perfect alignment. A line can be dropped with a small lead shot attached to the end through all the guides as another alignment check.

e. Guides that are not in alignment can be gently wiggled and moved into proper alignment if the winding thread has not been wound too tightly.

f. Move the guides only a little at a time. Make sure that after each guide has been moved, the foot of each guide is still flat against the rod surface .

g. Continue this procedure until all of the guides are in perfect alignment.

h. Check the alignment again by turning the rod over so that the guides are now hanging on the bottom of the rod and look down the rod through the guides.

i. Mount your reel in the reel seat and make certain that the reel also aligns with the guides. If the reel is not in alignment

Figure 17-9
Aligning the Guides

with the guides it will only be necessary to change the alignment of the guides on the bottom portion of the rod as the upper section can be brought into alignment by rotating the rod at the ferrule.

9. Decorations

a. To further decorate your rod you may wish to put one-half inch to one inch of winding thread at the end of the top guide, from each end of the ferrule, and from the end of the handle. Custom rod builders often put a hook keeper at the end of the handle. One of the snake fly rod guides removed from the rod can be used as a hook keeper.

b. After all windings are complete, use the handle of your pen knife or other instrument to rub across the thread windings and smooth each winding in place.

c. Sign and date your rod just above the handle with a fine tip silver or gold permanent marking pen. A custom built rod is a personal creation. A part of its beauty is the signature of its creator. An unsigned Stradivarius violin would not give the pleasure that a signed and dated one would provide.

10. Color Preservative.

a. Using your fingers or a small artist brush apply a liberal coat of color preservative to all thread windings.

b. Wait one hour between coats and apply a second and third coat of color preservative to all rod windings.

11. Rod Finishing

a. Apply at least two coats of a good rod varnish or rod finish.

b. The rod finish can be applied with a lint-free cloth, artist brush, or your fingers. The preferred method of applying varnish is using your fingers as the fingers rub the rod varnish or other finish into any nicks and scratches of the rod surface.

c. Make certain that the rod varnish or other finish covers all of the threads and windings.

d. The second varnish coat should be applied no sooner than 24-hours after the first coat.

e. Allow the rod finish to dry for at least 48 hours before using.

HAPPY FISHING!

Fly-and-Bubble Supplies

Bubbles

12 Bubbles	$6.00
2 ounces Bubble Shot	.95
Shipping and handling	3.00
Total	**$9.95**

Book Special

Fish Don't Think	$18.00
3 Bubbles	1.50
1 "Little Green Fly"	1.75
1 ounce of Bubble Shot	.50
Shipping (Priority Mail) and handling	5.00
Total value	$27.75
Special Only	**$19.95**

Quanity	Item	Price each	Total
_____	Bubbles	9.95	_____
_____	Book & Bubbles	19.95	_____
	Total		_____

Send Name and Address with check or money order payable to:

Fish Don't Think
P.O. Box 6012
Longmont, CO 80501

Prices subject to change without notice.

Flies
Specially tied flies designed for Fly-and-Bubble fishing
(All flies are $1.95 each)

Flies	*Quanity*
Little Green Fly	_____
Wolly Bugger	_____
Hornberg	_____
Maribou Adams	_____
Black Midge	_____
Black Ant	_____
Nymph	_____
Black Maribou Streamer	_____
Maribou Wing Royal Coachman	_____
Total number of flies	_____

Number of flies _____ x $1.95 each =   _____
Shipping and handling   3.00
                                        Total   _____

Send Name and Address with check or money order payable to:

Fish Don't Think
P.O. Box 6012
Longmont, CO 80501

Prices subject to change without notice.